If not now –
When?

A story about Geoff, a gentleman who fell down the stairs.

First published 2015 by DB Publishing, an imprint of JMD Media Ltd,
Nottingham, United Kingdom.

ISBN 9781780915104

Printed and bound in the UK by Copytech (UK) Ltd Peterborough

If not now – When?

A story about Geoff, a gentleman who fell down the stairs.

Annie Fielder

This book is dedicated to Will Smith –
a man of immeasurable kindness whose humble nature
would not let me thank him in person – so this
book is written in thanks to you.

Contents

Foreword

No planning permission was ever requested for my professional wall but it has been quietly constructed over the past few years, silently doing its job of sheltering me from the painful elements of a sudden loss by trauma, stroke or infection, or the slow stealing by dementia or MS. The advance is insidious: people become patients. It starts with not dwelling on a patient dying, but quickly builds to a death, meaning one less job that day. Whilst that didn't go unnoticed, I wrote off the inherent inhumanity as necessary to get through the day without blubbing like a fountain.

I first met Geoff at the Derby City General Hospital (now The Royal Derby Hospital) during his admission to King's Lodge Neurological Rehabilitation Unit for a brain injury. Despite his condition, his charm, heart for his family and his passion for singing were so evident.

It was no single picture that broke me, but together, their beautiful and concerted effort dismantled my professional wall to see the literal points of view of Geoff and those who held him dear. These warm and engaging pictures concisely capture a story of loss and remains and love. The sudden, the attrition and the enduring.

Back on the wards, I am not blubbing. It turns out Annie didn't totally dismantle the wall: she just put in some very large windows.

Tim Hardman. Derbyshire NHS.
Speaking about the exhibition of the project about Geoff which led to this book.

Acknowledgements

Crowdfunding donors:
Pauline Cobley. Charlie Fielder. Claire Page. Margaret Shermer. Charlotte Kay. Wendy Singleton. David Moss. Emma Ward. Simon Hall. Charlie Reeson. Rob Colquhoun. Hayley Flood. Paul Roberts. Sylvia Ibraham. James Davidson. Tom McMahon. Kathy and Rob Henderson. Simon Thorne. Samantha Diston. Nick Jones. Enid Ruff. Jennie Beck. Sally Henniker-Major. Jayne Anders. Will Smith. Roy and Eva Tuff. Catherine Robson. Emily Douce. Vicki Astle. Sarah Suggitt. Karen Lomax. Robin Newman. Ashley Scott-Minns. Wilbur Henderson. Jord Scott-Minns. Anna Forsberg. Gill and Michael Grace. Anita Astle. Be Payne. Mary Boocock. Chris Saunders. Nick and Deryn Walker. Mary Burrows. Helen and Peter Jones. Stephanie Kent. Jon Thorne. Bex Bennett. Seb Chaudhry. Clara Burn. Vipul Thakrar. Kika and Chris Dabbs. Adrian Daley. Lyndsey Henderson. Gemma Wilkie. Antony Grace. Julia Hawkesford. Gillian Raine. Anne Giles. Lucy Dalgleish. Hermione. Cat Shore. Jenny Richardson. Simon Walker. Sarah Thorne. Paddy Fielder. Rosemary Shepard. Paul Clark. Helen Lewis. Emma Birrell. Tracey Pilling. Emily Wood. Michele Logsdon. Elizabeth Henshaw. Alex Atkin. C Blackwell. Sally Casboult. Ruthie Beach. Julie Cox. Laura Kendrick-Harrison. Jenny Casboult. Dan Astle. Nat Fahy. Jack Cartledge. Fazane Fox. Andy Henderson. Friends of Geoff.

With special thanks to:
All of the staff at The Old Lodge, especially Matron, you are a wonderful force to be reckoned with.

Steve Caron of JMD Media Ltd for being terribly patient with me after I realised that writing a book immediately after having my first child was impossible and waiting without provocation.

The Derby Royal Hospital for dealing with our complaint with respect, kindness and understanding.

To Cath Robson for taking the time to sit up late check and edit this book in fine detail for me, repeatedly, without complaint or making me feel foolish. You are an extremely lovely lady - thank you!

My sister Kathy Henderson for taking the time to edit this book despite being a very busy doctor lady and mother and for, more importantly, being there with me on that terrible day – you saved me.

My business partner and loyal friend Rachel Pratt for letting me take Whiffle Pig off in a completely new direction, working with people with Head Injuries and supporting my wild ideas and adventures. You are the epitome of a true friend and I'm sorry I am like a confusing whirlwind in the workplace.

My mother Jenny Casboult, my mother in law Anita Astle and my husband Daniel Astle for supporting me completely whilst I wrote this book. For coming to sit with my little boy so I could work upstairs knowing he was safe and never complaining (especially when I made you a three minute lunch out of things I found in the kitchen) and never making me feel guilty when I always took longer than I planned. You are incredible – I feel so lucky to have your constant support and will always be grateful you gave me this time.

Introduction.

====

When this first happened to us, we couldn't find any reading matter or information about our situation. There were the obligatory pamphlets dotted about the hospitals but they were all very clinical. From quite early on in our experience, I decided that I wanted to be able to use what had happened to us to help other people who also found themselves at a similar life changing junction. *'If not now – When?'* was the title of Geoff's life story that he had started to write before he lost his ability to continue it. He took the well known Hebrew saying "If I am not for myself, who will be for me? And when I am for myself, what am 'I'? And if not now, when?" I have helped him finish it. In using his originally planned title, it still makes it Geoff's book.

The intention was not to shock or offend anyone reading it, but to open the door to the reality of a situation like ours. Real photos and detailed descriptions of the events have been used so that you, the reader, can really place yourselves in our position and, perhaps, relate. I wanted to find a way to increase the support for family members who have found themselves acting as carers. I want people to see the pressures the NHS staff are under and help them to communicate properly with one another. I wanted to make death and the people it has recently touched, something that should not necessarily be feared. Death is an inevitable part of life. This is our story.

This is how it happened for us and we hope that sharing it can bring some comfort, and perhaps a bit of laughter to others during their darker times.

"To fear death, gentlemen, is no other than to think oneself wise when one is not, to think one knows what one does not know. No one knows whether death may not be the greatest of all blessings for a man, yet men fear it as if they knew that it is the greatest of evils."

— Socrates

1.

The man before
the head injury

═══════════

THIS is a story about Geoff. He was my stepfather. On 23rd September 2008 he fell down the stairs, which resulted in a large head injury. It was unknown if he had a stroke which led to the fall; or a fall which led to the stroke. We will never know as he could never remember.

Before I start this story, I want to tell you about the man before the accident because it is important that he is documented and remembered for the 65 years he existed without the head injury.

Geoff was a husband, a father, a stepfather, an electrical engineer, an intellectual, a kind man, a witty man, a depressed man, a tall man and – above all – a gentleman, and boy… did he love music. My childhood was bound in music and that is with thanks to my parents.

Geoff grew up in Long Eaton, Derbyshire with his older brother Michael and his mother and father. He was always a very keen musician, as was his brother; with both of them being members of the local church choir. Michael was a dab hand at guitar, piano and organ and Geoff played the drums. It was evident from a young age that Geoff was an intellectual. Being the only one in his family going on to higher education, this bothered his mother; he noted in his writings about his life that his mother had once said, "People like us do not do things like that." His mother, Kath, worked in the hosiery factory CoxMoore and his father was a painter and decorator; a skill Geoff absorbed and he was often keen to start a new project on a room in the house when we were young (although he often strayed near completion when another room was giving him the eye.) Geoff's mother often belittled Geoff as she feared that Michael would feel inferior to him as he wasn't as smart nor as handsome, so she wanted to bring Geoff down to make Michael feel better about himself. Michael didn't feel this way; he was very close to Geoff and happy with himself. Michael and his mother were very similar and enjoyed their routine and didn't like to sway from it, whereas Geoff and his father were go getters; his father dreamed of owning a detached house which his mother thought to be ridiculous.

When Geoff was 18, his father had a fatal heart attack aged 46. Dying at such a young age haunted Geoff and he saw it as a sign that he too would die at 46. As it happened he outlived the age of all of his little family but not with the grace and dignity that he would have envisaged. Geoff and Michael decided to make a pact to never leave their mother alone at home, taking it in turns to go out so the other could stay in with her. In time Geoff began courting a girl called Ellen so Michael slipped into staying in all the time so that Geoff could see more of Ellen. They would exchange love letters and arrange to meet for tea at each other's homes; all terribly 1950's. Ellen was a sweet and nervous girl and Geoff's soft and gentle nature warmed her.

After time they married. It was at this point they decided to move to Suffolk. This was where they met my mother and father and became good friends. Mum and Dad actually gazumped them on a house they had wanted called Peppercorn Cottages, which was my first home. Michael decided to remain at home with their mother so she would never be alone. Michael didn't have any relationships at any time and it was unknown if he was homosexual, uncomfortable with coming out or just totally disinterested in relationships.

Despite Geoff being a talented jazz drummer he decided to pursue the life of a family man rather than a musician. His love of percussion never left him and he would drum on every surface he could find, be it the dining room table, the steering wheel or the top of our heads. Sadly, in spite of years of trying he and Ellen did not fall pregnant. They had a handsome Labrador called Sam whom they loved and started to admit defeat about children. It became evident that Ellen's anxious nature was growing ever more disabling. She became increasingly agoraphobic and her anxiety made life quite hard for her and Geoff. Ellen kept little diaries, with just a few lines on each page. The entries were very regimented; always documenting the weather and her mood. Geoff would comment that if they ever went out anywhere, Ellen would often retreat to the sanctuary of their Saab.

In April 1984 Ellen found a lump in her breast, which turned out to be cancer. Ellen had surgery to remove the lump 10 days later then started treatment immediately, all of this was marked in her diary in a very matter of fact way. After the surgery, the doctors spoke to them both saying that they had got all of the cancer and she would be fine stating: "All of her organs are clear." After recovering they both went to visit their own GP for a check up and recounted what the hospital doctor had told them with relief. At this point their GP's face dropped and he said, "Didn't they tell you? When they opened you up they saw the cancer had spread to all of your organs… You only have a few months left." Apparently, upon performing the surgery they had seen the awful state of her cancer riddled organs and then just closed her up again (common practice back then for the surgeons to leave the dirty work to the family GP). Ellen died two weeks later in the February of 1985. She woke Geoff up in the middle of the night and said, "Can you help me please?" and he replied, "Of course." He said she then made a small gurgling noise and died in his arms. Geoff called the doctor and the undertaker and then sat downstairs on his own.

This was the reason why Geoff did not trust doctors and held resentment towards them. This was the reason why he would not go to the doctors until he was physically vomiting blood and why he wouldn't even take paracetamol for a headache and this was one of the main reasons that he fell down the stairs that night.

Some time later, my sisters Charlie, Kathy and I moved to

Derbyshire to live with Geoff following our parents' separation. We lived in Thorpe in the Peak District. Life was very happy for us and my father soon met a lovely lady called Sarah who had four boys so I gained brothers too. Life was sometimes difficult but memories were of silliness and laughter.

We had posh dinners in the dining room on a Saturday night where we were permitted fizzy pop courtesy of the old Soda Stream, which used to honk like a goose when it had reached maximum fizziness. One evening Geoff came down dressed as his imaginary girlfriend 'Flossy', donning one of Mum's dresses and a fine looking flappy hat which housed a rather flaccid and sorry for itself flower. He spent the entire meal posing as Flossy smearing his lipstick on his wine glass. I laughed until I was nearly sick. This was good stuff to a 5-year-old. He really made my mother laugh. Mum laughed all the time in those days.

We had remained close to Ellen's mother. Sadly Ellen's father died a few weeks after Ellen's death, so Mum and Geoff felt it important to always involve her mother. We all called her Auntie Doris and her house smelt like flowers and she would let me eat little cut up Frankfurter sausages by the gas fire.

In 1989 Auntie Doris called Geoff and asked him to come round after work, she had discovered a lump in her breast and, also being nervous of doctors, asked Geoff if he would check it for her to see if it felt like what Ellen had. Geoff, being the irrevocably kind gentleman that he was, did what must have been very upsetting and uncomfortable for them both. I can only imagine that he did it in the most dignified and sensitive way. Sadly, like her daughter, Auntie Doris did have breast cancer and she died a short time after.

Not long after my mother, being the most fertile woman in Britain, was able to give Geoff something that he had always wanted: in the summer of 1989 my little sister Sally rolled up and we were all totally enamoured with her, no one as much as Geoff. He completely doted on her. Sally really looked like him too with her sandy hair, bright blue eyes and one dimple in her right cheek.

Sadly, in 1991 Geoff's mother had a heart attack whilst walking in the street and had died by the time she had hit the floor. Geoff and Michael went to identify the body. He later spoke of how her face was bruised and her glasses smashed so she must have landed face first to the ground. Before Sally's birth we had always referred to her as 'Auntie Kath', so it was lovely for her to have been a real Grandma for that short amount of time.

Almost exactly a year later, Michael had a heart attack whilst cleaning his car. His neighbour found him in the garage. My mother received a phone call from a neighbour saying that he had been taken away in an ambulance and she then spent the rest of the day calling all the hospitals in the area trying to track him down. Not being a blood relative made this much more difficult as the nurses were unable to say anything coupled with the fact that Michael had no identification on him when he died so Mum had to describe him. This took so much longer as he looked much older than his 52 years. Eventually it was deduced that he had died instantly and Mum had to call Geoff at work to tell him, she doesn't remember the conversation in detail except that Geoff responded with, "Oh God – not Michael too. He was my pal." He then had to go and identify his brother alone. To make matters worse, the papers put a call out for the unclaimed body of Michael Casboult, which the family read whilst planning for the funeral. This upset Geoff deeply as Michael, quite clearly, had been claimed and loved.

Michael, as well as being a talented musician, was also an incredibly gifted craftsman. He made beautiful models to an exquisite level of detail; such as a minute wick for a 5mm candle to go atop a small hand crafted table. When clearing the house in the weeks following the funeral (which was an arduous task as they liked to keep stuff, them Casboults) we came across a simple newspaper clipping of a pin-up girl. Nothing seedy or pornographic, but it just showed that he *had* been interested but it had never happened for him other than in hope. Geoff's heart was crushed; this was the beginning of his deep depression and the always happy and laughing Geoff began to crumble away.

Not wanting to involve doctors in any way he did not seek any help for his depression and withdrew all his pain inside himself. We would still see 'Good Geoff' but his visits became less frequent as the years went on.

Geoff's depression began to consume him bit by bit and it was as though someone was slowly pulling a blackout blind over our home. There was only one thing in the world which would bring him out of his darkness, no matter how deep, and that was Sally. Even after the accident when he was having the worst of his days, Sally would just have to walk in the building and his face would light up and he would be alright again for the time that she was in the room. Sally was the best thing he ever did and he did everything in his power to never let her see him upset or act angry in front of her. Ironically, his behaviour then affected the way Sally dealt with him after his accident. Because of his previous determination to shield her from anything he deemed scary or dark, she found it completely overwhelming when his illness meant he was unable to control his emotions or behaviour and often couldn't bear to be anywhere near him. His attempts to keep her close and protect her ultimately pushed her away from him completely leaving them both deeply hurt.

He was not so precious with the rest of us, especially Mum and me. Due to the fact I had been so little when my parents divorced, I had become a very confused, troubled and needy child. I suffered terribly with night terrors and bed wetting which, unfortunately, meant the whole household also did. Many a night I would wake up to see Mum, Geoff, Kathy and Charlie all standing in my room blinking at me through baggy eyes after I had woken them all with my horrific screaming. It was not an easy role for Geoff to slide into and, since I was so small, I would always ask for my dad, especially when scared.

I remember that my bedroom door had a funny doorknob that would sometimes fall off. One time, when I was about six, the door handle came off from the inside when I was in the room. Instantly I became frightened and started to bang on the door. It was the weekend so everyone was either downstairs or in the garden – somewhere pottering as families do at the weekend, so no one heard me. This led to me becoming utterly terrified at the feeling of being trapped and not being able to get to my Mum who I needed more than ever. Eventually Geoff must have heard me and opened the door. By this point I was past the point of no return and in total hysteria. Geoff, having little tolerance for me any way and not quite knowing what to do, slapped me hard across the face. It worked. I stopped screaming. I do not remember much after that apart from Mum cuddling me and carrying me down the stairs. I remember as we walked past their bedroom Geoff was lying down on the bed. He did not get up again for a long time, I remember it being days, but I imagine it was just a couple of hours. Apparently, just after it happened, I whimpered that I wanted to talk to my Daddy, which cannot have helped.

That was the only time something like that happened and I only tell you about this not to make you form a bad opinion of him, but because it comes back later in his life and literally haunted him. Geoff was a very gentle creature and I accept that dealing with a tornado of terrified toddler is enough to throw anyone off their toes, especially one that is not used to such a thing.

When Geoff was good, and all the time before the darkness, he would make me laugh and show incredible thoughtfulness. But when the darkness lurked he could be cruel in his words and his amazing ability to always make me laugh would do the opposite. It was such a shame that such a strong and happy gentleman was brought down to his knees by such an awful disease.

As the years went on life would fluctuate between the darkness and light and sometimes you could see the darkness coming and sometimes you couldn't. It was the same when it went away; some days it would dissipate gradually and some days it would just be gone and it would be sunny again. During those dark days he would walk into the room and it would feel sharp and prickly and his face would look stern; Geoff had very wild eyebrows which often needed to be tamed by his hairdresser and they were very expressive, so his angry eyes were very fierce indeed but his happy eyes soft and warm. I remember thinking how out of control his eyebrows were at the end; like great thickets balancing on top of very frightened eyes. Mum would often threaten to 'go at them' much like she did with our bedraggled hair as teenagers, pursuing us about the house making scissor gestures with her fingers.

Mum and Geoff had a wonderful relationship at the start. There was a great deal of laughter and silliness in our home. Camping trips to Clumber Park and to Brittany in France; playing ball games like 'Three Bad Eggs' until the sun went down and hours upon hours of driving to and from those places. The car was filled to the brim with music either blasting out of the stereo from a ready made mix tape that one of us girls had baked the night before or bellowing from our mouths. On one particular good day there was a fine combination of both: from our house in France to the beautiful town of St Malo was just a short 45 minute car journey but it crossed a bridge that would lift to let boats through. On this particular day the bridge was up so we were in a long stream of traffic waiting to go again, when *The Frog Chorus* by Paul McCartney came next on the tape. Instantly we all sprang into full-bellied song. Mum, Geoff, Charlie, Sibby (Charlie's best friend who frequented most family holidays with us), Kathy, Sally and I were not timid in the art of song, so were pelting out our parts with emphatic charge. Geoff taking his role as the fat frogs with great seriousness as Kath embodied the large fish bursting out of the water; a tear jerking performance. When we crescendoed the finale with mighty force there was a moment's silence then an eruption of applause and cheers from all of the cars surrounding us in the queue; huge smiles and whistles from our adoring fans just as the bridge came down and we all started to set off again. In my life now, whenever I have to face something difficult or frightening, I close my eyes and think about that moment. The tears of laughter glossing everyone's eyes, Geoff's broad smile preventing him from properly finishing his sentence, the frantic clapping from the French strangers who had enjoyed the show, the glorious sunshine and the strong comforting warmth of total happiness beaming from everyone in that car. I am probably the only person in the world who cries when they hear *The Frog Chorus*.

We lived in Thorpe, in The Peak District and we had lovely warm summers where we would play down in the valley near our house and cold snowy winters where the electricity would go out for days and we would sledge until our undergarments were soaked through and then huddle together whilst Geoff toasted us crumpets one at a time on the open fire in the living room. When I was about five or six – before Sal was born, Geoff woke me. He told me he wanted me to hear the most beautiful sound in the world. It must have been about 9 or 10pm in the height of summer as the sun was just setting and he carried me out into the garden wrapped in my duvet. "Look up onto the chimney stack – can you see that blackbird? He has found the highest point in the garden to sing for his territory and claim our garden as his. There is another blackbird over there on the neighbour's roof – do you see? Now listen, listen to their bird song – isn't that just beautiful?" I can still remember looking up and seeing the silhouette of the blackbird and listening to its song and feeling totally safe and comfortable. I fell asleep in his arms listening to that elegant song. The very early years were sweet and lovely.

So that was Geoff: extremely funny, kind and warm but also soaked entirely in sadness. As time went on, the sadness started to fill him more and would drip from him leaving angry bitter pools about the place. By the time he had his accident he was almost entirely coated in sadness all the time. He used to call me on Sunday mornings for a little catch up chat which would last for an hour or two but the chats became less frequent and seeing him had become difficult as he would be so sharp and scratchy. Mother, on the other hand, was always an enormous smiley hug with splashes of dinner cast about the place: dependable, hilarious and the strength of the bear.

Geoff, Uncle Michael and their mother as young boys.

Geoff, Uncle Michael and their father as young boys.

John and Kath Casboult
(Geoff's parents)

Geoff and Uncle Michael as
teenagers with their father who
looks notably older than his age,
which was early 40s.

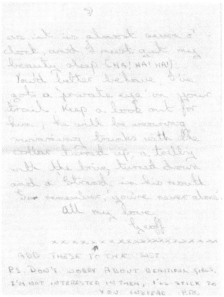

Geoff recording for Radio
4 with his jazz band in the
mid 60s.

Love letter from Geoff to Ellen
when they were courting, showing
Geoff's silly kind heart and Ellen's
insecurities.

Geoff and Ellen's wedding day. (Geoff's Mother, Geoff, Ellen,
Uncle Michael, Ellen's Mother, Ellen's Father.)

Ellen with her father who
died two weeks after her of
a broken heart.

Earl Soham, Suffolk. Late 70s.

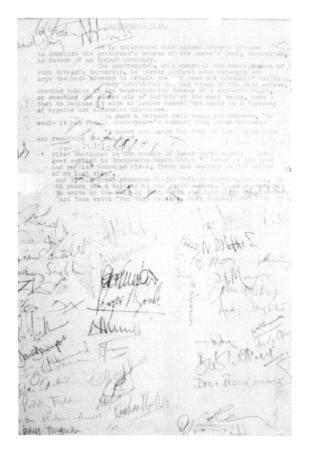

Silly petition, signed by my dad and Geoff, still up in the gentlemen's toilets at The Queen's Head in Brandeston, Suffolk.

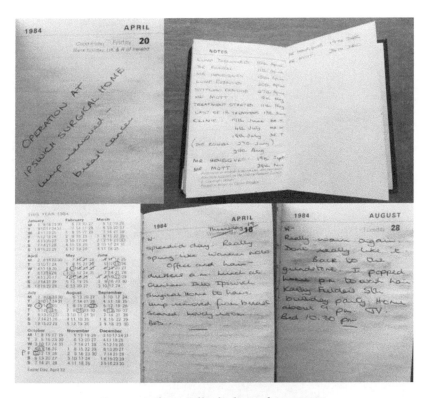

Excerpts from Ellen's diary from 1984.

*Geoff and Ellen on holiday
in the late 70s.*

*Sitting in the back of 'Mustard'
the Volvo estate outside
Springfield House. Kath, me,
Charlie, Mum and Sam.*

Uncle Michael never left their mother until the day she died.

Divorced family bliss. Dad carrying me, with Kathy, Charlie and Geoff about to head up Thorpe Cloud in search for Father Christmas in his fat leotard (something I had decided and often encouraged jaunts to catch him out up there)

Mum and Geoff's wedding day. Me showing my fury at the dress I didn't like by defiantly pulling a face.

1987 in Thorpe, pre Sal, with the Lewises.

Geoff with Sally 1989.

Mum, Geoff and Sal in Erquy 1991.

Geoff on a good day, looking happy.

Geoff with his first grandchild Maddie.
He loved being a 'Papa', 2005.

'Come and play in the sand, Papa', 2008.

2.

Moving a wardrobe
down a flight of stairs

IN mid September 2008 Geoff had been really poorly with a Urinary Tract Infection (UTI). He had taken time off work, which, for him, was a rarity. He always found some way to work and would work himself into the ground; one of the main reasons he was so ill in the first place. He had popped round to see me erecting my new shed in the garden a few days before and he had brought his black dog with him as he was full of snipey remarks and cold stares. That was the last time I would see him before his accident.

Due to Geoff's inherent distrust of doctors he had put off seeking medical help for as long as possible; just choking down 'one paracetamol' in an attempt to feel better. He did finally go to the doctors and was prescribed some antibiotics. He didn't appear to be getting better, and, in fact, became a good deal worse. Mum decided to sleep in the spare room as Geoff, a long term insomniac, would be more easily disturbed with her in the bed with him.

Very early on the morning of 23rd September Mum was woken at 2am by a loud banging sound and went to investigate. In my parents' house the stairs go up and then turn to the left then split off in opposite directions. Mum and Geoff's room is to the right up nine steps and then, to the left, three steps lead to 'the girls' bedrooms plus bathroom and spare room. Mum found Geoff sprawled at the bottom of that sort of T-junction. Being the wise woman that she is she decided to phone my sister Kathy, who had just qualified as a Doctor. She said, "Geoff's fallen down the stairs. He's unconscious. He's making ever such a weird noise – listen," then held the phone up to his crumpled face so Kathy could hear the rapid raspy breaths he was making. As soon as Mum put the phone back to her ear Kathy said "Mum – call the ambulance immediately, don't call me!" So she did.

Apparently the speed of his breathing meant that something was very wrong and more importantly, he was unconscious at the bottom of a small flight of stairs in the middle of the night. Mum waited patiently for the ambulance; being slightly out in the sticks it is always a struggle for people to find the house but they made it. Due to the awkwardness of the staircase coupled with Geoff's six foot plus height and dead weight Mum said it was like watching two people manoeuvring a wardrobe down a flight of stairs. It turned out to be the last time Geoff ever went down those stairs again.

They both travelled to the Derby Royal Infirmary where they then tried to wake Geoff. The doctors asked Mum to try as she would have a voice he recognised, they were right and her voice managed to rouse him. They asked him if he knew where he was and he managed to say "hospital" before passing out again, so Mum felt happy that there was some hope. After a scan of his head they could see there was a bleed on his brain, they were unsure if the bleed had caused the fall or the fall had caused the bleed and hoped that Geoff would be able to shine some light on the subject upon waking. He was transferred to Queen's Medical Centre in Nottingham for brain surgery to stop the bleed. At that point, the diagnosis was a Subarachnoid Haemorrhage, which is very serious.

This was when Kathy called me, at around 5:45am. I remember the call clearly: "Annie – don't panic but something has happened to Geoff. He has fallen down the stairs and is in hospital, it is pretty serious, he is having surgery. We are driving down now and Mum is already at the hospital."

I had to wait an hour for someone to be able to give me a lift as I couldn't drive at that point, so I busied myself with making up a care package for everyone who was going to be at the hospital and every possible scenario for what they may or may not want. Since all of the sisters would be coming and Charlie had a three-year-old this proved a very handy task as it was both time-consuming and distracting. I packed snacks for small people, snacks for older people, snacks for Mum (she likes her sandwiches in a certain way) drinks of all varieties, stupid magazines with stories of people who are always much worse off than you no matter how bad things get, tampons, sanitary towels, pants liners (just in case), plasters and small medical whatnots such as paracetamol etc (just in case), deodorant and dry shampoo as most of us upped and hot-footed it to the hospital so did not have time to assess the cleaning situation, pencils and paper, fishing tackle etc; everything for every possible scenario in the entire world. I came tearing down the Queen's Med corridors, panting desperately as I lumbered around what seemed like hundreds of sharp corners giving the illusion that I was just going around in circles before bursting into the waiting room of intensive care looking like a very sweaty version of The Junk Lady from *Labyrinth* to find a rather watery-eyed Mum being comforted by Sally.

The waiting room was very small for the number of chairs it had in it. About 13 feet square with chairs you can't sleep in, even if you really tried, lined up around the edge. There were about seven posters of different sizes with writing on them on the walls and I decided that I would save reading them for later as we were going to be there for a while. Mum informed me that he was "in surgery now, we have no idea how long it will be and he will either come out and wake up and be normal, come out and wake up and have a totally different personality or not come out at all". Then she sobbed for a little bit and I decided that the best thing for me to do was to log that bit of information and deal with the potentially grizzly outcome when and if it happened and just deal with what was happening as it was happening and support anyone who needed it. This was the way I dealt with everything from that day on.

As time passed, we all chatted and Mum laughed at the variable contents of my bags and after a little while Kathy bouldered in followed by Charlie and her husband Daren and their three-year-old daughter Maddie. Soon we had taken over that small waiting room with our less than discreet cackles of laughter used as protective shields to hide the sheer terror which either outcome offered us.

I don't know who told us his surgery was a success or even when; in fact I remember none of that. I just remember going into the Intensive Care Unit for the first time and Kathy warning me, "He looks weird because he doesn't have his glasses on and he always looks more angry without his glasses." Then walking past two beds, each with two nurses standing guard and a spaghetti junction of wires and tubes weaving about their person; both robots having the air puffed into them in perfect synchronisation. At the end of the room was a third robot with a large bandage on his head like Mr Bump and that was Geoff. Eyes closed, mouth open and chest rising and falling in a sharp lurch accompanied by the 'puff/hiss' of the lung machine. Criticallly ill, but alive.

To accompany the large head injury/possible stroke and huge brain surgery, he also had septicaemia and mild pneumonia. The sepsis, it turned out, was a result of the UTI not being treated with the correct antibiotics. This was in no way an error of his general practitioner, it just sometimes takes time to find the right course to suit the infection. As Geoff had left it so long before going to the GP it had infected his blood. We then started to piece together that he may have tried to walk to their ensuite bathroom and gone out of the wrong door because he was so unwell and that resulted in his short jaunt down the stairs. This was loosely the story we always stuck with as to what had happened.

He was unable to cough because he was in an induced coma so the staff would force his body to cough up the gunk on his lungs by pushing a tube down his throat, (which is as revolting as it sounds and

I shan't go into too much of a detailed description only to say there was enough of it to collect in a lovely transparent bucket by his bed). This in turn made his body turn a delectable shade of puce and he would seize up. It was not a nice sight and was pretty sodding down right scary but I was with Sally when I saw this and it made her burst into tears so I held onto to her and turned her away and explained it as it was happening, so she knew what was happening as she wanted to know he was okay. Afterwards, as his body returned to the healthy pale shade it had taken on over the past week, I distracted Sal with cheerful stories and by pointing out that the contents of the bucket (excess brain fluid which was being removed via a shunt) was reminiscent of peach schnapps. Sally was very grateful for this observation and noted that Archers used to be her favourite drink. I do not think she has drunk it since.

We all moved up one floor to the large restaurant and made it our base for the days to follow as it was just a short walk (down the corridor, first door on the left, down one flight of stairs and through the doors) to the ICU and there was much more room for us to sprawl out and then we could take it in turns to visit Geoff as we were only allowed in two at a time. It is strange that all I remember was laughter during this time. Laughter at the state of my hair/clothes/general battered demeanour, laughter at Mum who (despite the directions back to the ICU being insanely easy) would give us a rather desperate call about 27 minutes later having found herself in the Ear, Nose and Throat department and not really very sure how she got there. Laughter at training little Madeleine to ask strangers if they had been for a wee or a poo as they came out of the toilet purely for our own amusement. Time did seem to fly.

These are some survival tips for if you ever find yourself having to stay in a hospital for any length of time all of a sudden:

- Expect to wait a LONG time – for everything – then wait a bit longer.
- No one talks to one another so be prepared to explain your situation to every new nurse/doctor who starts their shift, of which there will be many as their 12 hour shifts will just go flying by. So maybe write a little note to put by the bed of your loved one so that you can leave knowing that the important things are noted down.
- Parking is EXPENSIVE but you can buy weekly/monthly tickets if you ask, which will save you a great deal of money.
- You can sometimes get a discount in the restaurant/canteen if you ask the sister on the ward to sign a note to prove that you are visiting a long term patient every day. It's not much but it is the same that the staff get.
- Practice extreme patience. As infuriating as it feels waiting for what seems like forever then discovering that the doctor had to dash off to another emergency so didn't have time to check on your family member – again – may seem like you are being royally dumped on, remember that the majority of these staff are utterly exhausted and often embarrassed at having to come and tell you these things and they will be very underpaid and overworked. So choose your battles wisely, as you may end up saying something you regret and you don't want to add internal guilt to your already stewing insides.
- Following that: keep a day to day diary of scans, names of doctors, what was said and when and any discrepancies or situations where you felt that you were wrongly treated and make sure you document the times where your care was outstanding and the staff kind – people seem to only speak up to complain and rarely

speak up to praise and hospitals benefit hugely from both types of feedback. All these little jottings will be helpful some days, weeks and years to come when you are speaking to a new doctor who will, more than likely, have had no chance at all to read through the vast notes of your loved one due to time restrictions. If you know what you are talking about and who you talked to it makes everything much easier to sort. This also gives you time, where you would ordinarily be sat staring and getting gradually more enraged, to reflect and write.

- Be respectful of everyone around you, including staff, as you may feel like your world is crashing down around you but it is often crashing down around everyone there, so a little smile or an offering of tea can make the day of a stranger who ends up being a friendly face when your sleep deprived eyes meet in the corridor at midnight a few weeks later.

- Do not hold back with your emotions if you need to cry then cry, staff will be used to that sort of thing and don't be afraid to laugh if something is funny. If you need to shout then go and shout. If you hold it all in, it all starts to build up inside you like unwanted gas which will inevitably come out when you don't want it to; like at a posh wedding. If you hold it all in you will end up bursting into tears when a stranger jumps in front of you in a queue at the supermarket or starting a fight with an elderly lady for 'looking at you wrong'. Go with the theory that everything is better out than in.

Tips for people whose friends and family have to visit someone in hospital for a long period of time:

- Only offer to give them lifts if you mean it, not just for a few visits. Their head will be so fully of worry and stress they won't want the added stress of worrying about who can give them lifts sometimes. This will save them the astronomical cost of parking and means they won't have to drive when they are mentally and physically exhausted.

- Don't be weird towards them. Talk to them completely normally. If they want to talk, just listen and offer advice *if* they ask. Talk to them normally, even if you think it's stupid and pointless, "I realised, after getting out of the car and walking in to meet you that my skirt was tucked into my pants and I passed *at least* 14 seriously ill patients." That sort of thing will make them laugh and pull them away from the swirling in their heads.

- If you find it difficult seeing them in person then just send them letters, e-mails, messages, parcels, a couple of times a week so they feel like they aren't forgotten.

- Dropping off food for them and only staying if they want you to or you feel comfortable with it.

- Anything you offer, offer with honest sincerity and not asking for a time limit as, often, hospital stays are unpredictably long and the 'out of sight, out of mind' theory soon kicks in to people not directly experiencing it. The person you are helping won't want you to feel put out and it will show if you are fed up of helping them regularly. Offer what you can do and offer what you want to do – even if it is offering a joke up via text message regularly, it is regular contact and care.

- Be kind and expect potential loss of contact from them. Not because they are annoyed or bored with you but because their mental capacity will go no further than the job at hand. Don't let this stop your contact, just be aware their lack of response isn't personal and they will trickle back when things get easier again.

- Don't freak out if they cry or scream in front of you. Don't freak out if you go into visit the person with them and they/the situation looks a bit scary but do talk to them about it afterwards as they may have been feeling the same and it might comfort them.

- Only ask how that person is if you really want to know the answer, only ask if you do care about them. People often ask if they are okay as they think they should then act awkward and make an excuse to be elsewhere which leaves that person feeling even worse.

Humans are resilient creatures. We quickly establish normality and routine in the most horrific of circumstances. No matter how bad situations immediately seem, they will change, be it for better or worse; they *will* change and we will be able to deal with that change when it comes. We're good like that.

26-09-03
Day 4   Intensive Care

Not knowing if he would survive at this point Mum drew Geoff. The ICU three days after his accident.

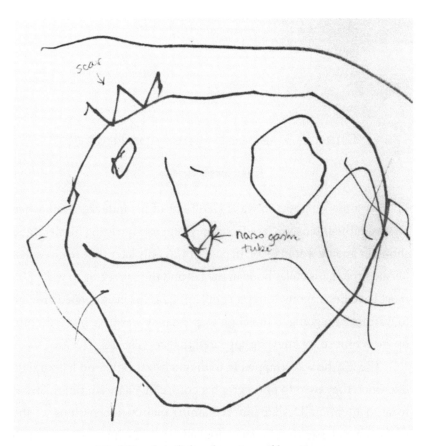

Maddie also did a drawing of her Papa.
Ironically, she drew it on a 'Cranium' pad.

3.

"Shall I start the applause?"

=================

IT took a few attempts to wake Geoff out of his induced coma when he was in the Intensive Care Unit; they kept on squeezing his neck and shoulder and he would recoil in pain. It was only later they realised that he had broken his collar bone in the fall and the squeezing to wake him must have been agony. After a couple of days his eyes opened enough to warrant him going to the High Dependancy ward; we had a thumbs up from him so we knew he appeared to recognise us.

The way he was strapped in to his chair was rather odd; bound up like when they used to photograph a corpse in Victorian times, forced to sit to attention. Despite him remaining mainly unconscious we still popped his glasses on him so he looked more like him and we bought a small MP3 player which we clipped onto his nightie. This played a mixture of songs so that, if he was in there at all, he wouldn't just be listening to the incessant beeps from his many machines.

His recovery was slow but evident. His eyes started to open and there was a flicker of recognition usually followed by deep chested sobs. Geoff had always been a man who was never able to cry if something had deeply upset him or he had been hurt by someone but would turn into a pool of water at a snifter of sweetness and love. The tsunami of love and support from everyone, but more importantly Mum and us, was too much for him to bear.

Over the following days he was moved from High Dependancy to a normal ward as his eyes were opening more and he was more respon-sive. Due to the tracheostomy he was still unable to speak but could mouth certain words. He clearly recognised us all and the friends who visited. The nurses had to strap his hands up with bandages like big child's mittens as he kept on wrenching out his NG tube in his sleep, so he would wave a mittened paw at you when you walked in with a little smile of recognition on his face. A Nasogastric 'NG' tube is a thin tube that goes down someone's nose, down their gullet and into their stomach so that they can be fed if they are unable to swallow.

It was decided that he would be transferred to the chest unit at the Derby Royal Infirmary as his pneumonia hadn't quite gone. This was the worst of our hospital stays. The DRI was on its way out at this point and many parts of the hospital had already moved on, leaving whole areas abandoned. The general state of the place was pretty dismal and the staff on the chest ward seemed frustrated and short tempered. The other downside to Geoff being on the chest ward was that everyone else was there *just* with chest problems. No one else had a serious head injury and it was very clear that the majority of the staff were not trained nor particularly interested in the extra care needed for him.

The main issue was him being far too hot. On many occasions we would arrive to see him bright red, sweating and distressed. When we asked the staff for help they were always too busy. Mum and I would soak towels in cold water and then lay them over his body and he would breathe out a sigh of instant relief and then he would relax. The worst example was when we came to find his bed covered in dried urine where he had wet the bed and it had gone unnoticed and had left to dry. This had happened because he had pulled out his catheter in his semi unconscious state (as he did with his NG tube) and no one had replaced it; each nurse blaming the other. At this point I was furious and said that it was totally unacceptable to find my parent lying in a bed of dried urine showing the level of neglect that was taking place. A young, and clearly embarrassed, male nurse helped us change the bed and sorted out a new catheter. Mum hadn't wanted me to stir up any problems with the people that were caring for him but this was not caring. It seemed blatantly clear to me that the staff were ready for the move up to the new hospital and had stopped seeing these patients as people. I realised then how easy it is for people to become desensitised to their jobs. Maybe it is easier to cope with, especially with the patients who are harder to handle or perhaps with the patients who are the sweetest, but then they die and it is too much to cope with; I am not sure but the robotic and cold care was evident everywhere and it was clear *something* needed to be done.

Care was a little better after that, primarily because we were there every day and I think I rattled their cages a bit. Things weren't always so dismal though. As a family we always try to see humour and light where we can. Mother took it upon herself to break into the cafeteria one evening as the hospital conveniently closed EVERYTHING at the weekends. With her drive taking an hour-and-a-half round trip and there being a two hour break between afternoon and evening visiting times, there was no point in her going home, but she still had to find time to catch up with her work so she prized open the doors to commandeer a table and chair so that she could mark all her school work in time. Ever resourceful, our mother.

The day came to remove the tracheostomy and we were all poised with tentative joy. After weeks of 'thumbs up' and the rock symbol we were eager to have Geoff back with his wit and kindness. When it was first removed Mum uttered, "Hello, my husband," in his ear and he took a deep breath and spoke in a very gravelly but clear voice: "Hello, my wife." At which we all poured onto the floor with great sobs. It was so lovely to hear him again.

About 30 minutes later we were sitting around chatting and Geoff gestured for Mum and I to come in closer so we could hear him speak. His eyes wide with sincerity, he whispered, "Shall I start the applause?" at which point Mum blinked several times and looked at me and said, "I beg your pardon? 'Start the applause?'" to which he nodded confidently as his eyes gazed around the room which contained three beds of rather old and ill ladies and gentlemen. "Well... if you like," Mum said and he seemed pleased with that. Mum then leaned into me and said: "We have all been waiting all this time for him to start talking...it never actually occurred to us that what he would say would be totally bonkers," and then fell into her usual wheezing fits of hysterical laughter.

And that is how things went on with Geoff's conversations: entirely lucid and normal one minute then, an in-depth discussion about how he was in Glasgow airport with Barack Obama. We all had great comfort in knowing that Geoff would have found this utterly hilarious.

Due to this dipping in and out of mild insanity, conversations often became... interesting. At this point it was mainly Mum and me every day as Charlie and Kathy had gone back home and were visiting WHEN THEY COULD and Sally was finding it difficult to visit because of the strange ways he had started to act. On one visit we were talking when he told us he really needed to urinate. We tried to get a nurse but there were none available and they were trying to get him to go himself rather than using a catheter. After five minutes of searching for help and Geoff becoming agitated saying he really had to go, Mum and I decided to tackle this ourselves. Having only a sick bowl to hand we pulled the curtain round and undid his trousers and helped him put his penis into the sick bowl so he could go. At this point he looked up with absolute horror. He looked at Mum, then at me, then at his penis and then back to us with this look of 'What in the world have you done THAT for?' so we said: "Well, don't you want a wee?" to which he loudly whispered "NO!" and looked at us like we were totally insane. At which point we dressed him, pulled back round the curtain then had to hide our mirth whilst he cast looks at us like we were naughty school children.

The aim was to treat Geoff's pneumonia so that he could get to King's Lodge Neurology Rehabilitation to really start to work on his head injury. We spent a couple of weeks in the DRI chest ward before being told there was a bed available.

My sketch of Geoff first time out in HD unit, propped up like a Victorian portrait of the dead.

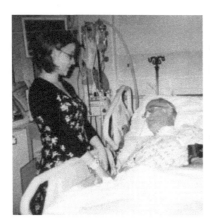

Geoff and Sally in Queen's Medical Nottingham.

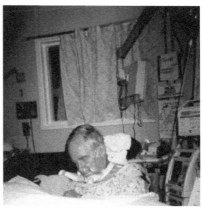

Geoff sitting up in Queen's Medical Nottingham.

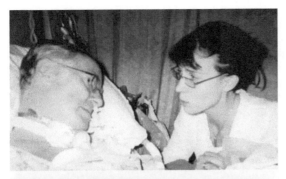

*Geoff and Charlie
having a serious
chat in the chest
unit DRI.*

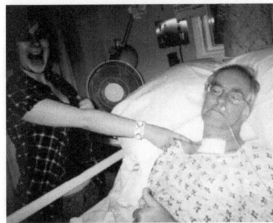

*The day the
tracheotomy
came out. Chest
unit DRI.*

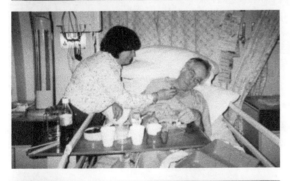

*Mum bringing
Geoff treats of
wine and cheese.*

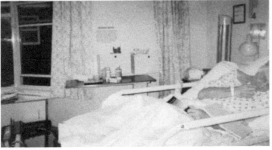

*The wild eyes he
would sometimes
have. Chest Unit
DRI.*

Looking a bit more like Geoff, with Sal, DRI

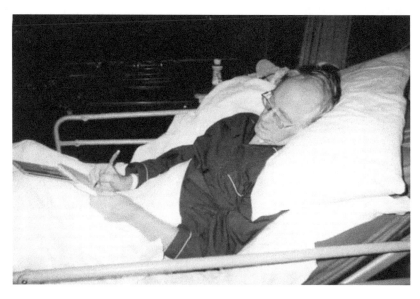

Attempting to write his name.

4.

King's Lodge

==========

DUE to renovations of the ward, King's Lodge was situated in temporary, single floored building in the car park of the Derby City General Hospital (now the Derby Royal Hospital). The atmosphere and attitude here was a world away from the DRI ward and we were so relieved. Geoff was in a big bay with an older gentleman called Ray and a younger gent called Colin. It turned out that Ray had gone to the same school as Geoff, but 20 years before him. He took him under his wing a bit and helped him. It was about this time that the wave of sadness hit. Geoff had suffered quite severely with depression, as I touched upon in the first chapter. This was predominantly due to him blocking out all the awful things he had experienced in the past; choosing to bury them rather than to deal with them. Something about the bang to his head made that no longer his decision, and it all came out. Head injuries can often make people unable to 'filter' or control how they feel and what they say. Almost every visit was met with great waves of emotion. Once (the bay empty and the curtains pulled round) I came to find Geoff hunched over in his chair consumed by shoulder-shaking sobs. One of the staff was trying to explain to me how it wasn't stopping; the room was dark and it was as though there was a storm caused by the grief that he had held inside for so long and now it was pouring down the walls and filling the floor up with tears. He cried for all of that day without stopping.

Upon my arrival one afternoon Geoff was enquiring as to how everyone in the family was, in a very lucid way, working through the family members and chatting about their comings and goings. Geoff always had a genuine interest and care in people and listened and remembered important things that mattered.

"How is Kath doing? Is she alright?"

"Kath's great – so busy in her first house job but calls loads to ask how you are."

"Yeah she called me the other day actually, sounded on good form…. How's Michael? Is he coming in to see me soon?

"Michael?"

"Yes Michael – my brother."

"Geoff. Michael is dead."

"What…. When did that happen?"

"Geoff, Michael died of a heart attack in 1992…."

"Did he? Oh no. He was such a dear man."

"Yes he was."

This happened every day after that for a while. He would ask where his brother Michael was and he would also ask about his labrador Sam who had died in 1987. Those were the only two he had forgotten had died. He knew his mother was dead despite her only dying a year before his brother. Each day we had to tell him that they had died and each day he heard it as if for the first time and would break down into great sobs. Sometimes I would come in to find him sobbing and he would croak, "Have you heard that Michael has died?" to me. It was a heartbreaking time for all of us. It soon became evident that Geoff's depression was beginning to have a very detrimental impact on his recovery.

It was about this time that we started with the little red book. This became an object of dependence and total trust for Geoff. He knew that if it was in the little red book it was true and it was definitely going to happen. Geoff's delusions of being in Scotland and in an airport were more commonplace now so we would write at the start of each week what the rota was for visitors and therapy and have a little list at the top which read something along the lines of:

"You have had a head injury.
You are not in Scotland.
You are not in an airport.
You are in Derby City Hospital near the Mallard Pub.
You cannot walk.
Your brother Michael died in 1992 and Sam died in 1987.
Jenny and the girls are at home and safe.
Nothing has changed to the house at home."

He often said that he could walk and had been walking around all night, he also worried that someone had changed the inside of his and Mum's house and become fretful about all of our safety. Mum had to change her answerphone message to a very deadpan recording: "Hello. I am either driving or on the telephone. I am fine. I will call you back when I have the chance". This was because he would call her all the time and if she didn't answer or it went to answerphone he would convince himself she had died and be beside himself, calling her over and over and then calling us.

We surrounded his bedside with photos of the garden and home so that he could see that nothing had changed and try to bring him comfort. Some days were better than others but he constantly worried that we were going to die. Maybe that worry had always been there for him, but since the depression had made him close down entirely before his accident we will never know. Perhaps all those people dear to him dying made him terrified that he would lose everyone who mattered to him? Maybe he thought it was something to do with him? Maybe he was scared of us meaning so much to him that he pushed us away so it wouldn't hurt him if we inevitably died? We will never know because he didn't talk about his depression before his accident, and he said he just didn't remember it afterwards. It was just the darkness in our home and he was still and silent during those times. He would often apologise for how he was now and we would say; "You were much worse before your accident!" and he would say: "Really? Was I? I can't remember being like that." Amazingly he just couldn't.

Perhaps he couldn't remember the darkness after his accident. He certainly never talked about it when he was 'him' again and he didn't apologise or want to make up for it. Other people I have known and met with depression speak about it as though it is their shadow and speak of it often. Geoff never spoke of it. It just consumed our home entirely when it was there and it was wonderful when it was gone again. Could it be that he just wasn't aware of it or just blocked it out as a way of coping with it? Another question which will remain unanswered for us forever.

Geoff remained fretful for his entire stay in hospital but became more lucid. He had the innocence of a worried little boy for most of the time and his role of parent to me seemed to vanish entirely. He seemed to look at me as one of the nurses, although he knew who I was. The way in which he spoke was as though I was one of his carers; which essentially I was. We had astounding support from all of the staff there and Geoff was having regular physiotherapy and occupational therapy. He also remained in good spirits about his rehabilitation; naming the rather unflattering and slightly demeaning hoist 'The Big Purple People Eater' and always joking with the staff and other in-patients. He was under the delusion that he could already walk so he did not push himself. Again the depression was the main factor in this; his clear denial. Although he was no longer convinced he was in Scotland[1] he did have little obsessions that he would talk about on a loop and we would have to calm him down and talk him round them. These little obsessions fluctuated but always remained after that.

---

1 *Reduplicate Paramneasia – People believing that one place or another (a country) has been duplicated or moved. Common after a head injury.*

It was decided after about three months, that he was unlikely to make any further progress. His rehabilitation had stayed the same and the doctors all agreed that the only thing stopping Geoff from walking was himself and the rest of the work would be up to him, with our support. It was time for him to come home. With a clearly typed out care plan and a temporary ramp made out of scaffolding, we brought him home.

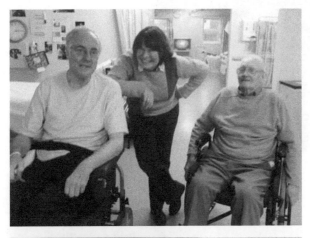

With Ray at Kings Lodge (sadly Ray died shortly after this was taken.)

With Sal at Kings Lodge looking normal again.

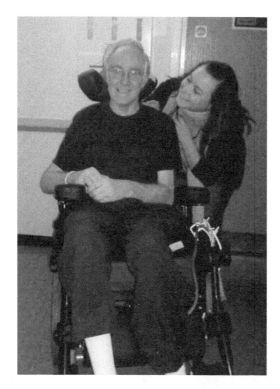

*With me having a
tour of Kings Lodge*

Kathy, Geoff and Sally at Kings Lodge.

*Having visitors at
Kings Lodge. Sitting
up straight, holding his
own head up.*

Christmas Day at Kings Lodge 2008.

Kings Lodge Christmas party with Mum and Sal.

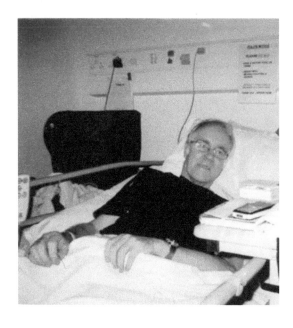

*Geoff looking
happy at Kings
Lodge.*

Geoff's red book.

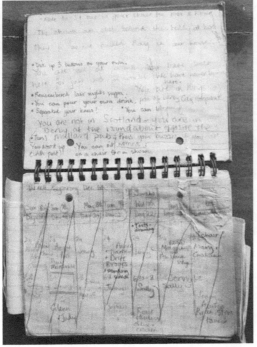

An example of a rather well weathered page in Geoff's red book. Showing his obsessions and people who were visiting when.

First trip home with Karl the OT trying out the new temporary ramp.

First trip home.

5.

Home again,
Home again Jiggity Jig

YOU always plan for things to be a certain way. You plan and you cover your plan and you prepare yourself for every possible outcome (a bit like giving birth). Your plan rarely pans out as you had prepared. That first night that Geoff came home was one of the hardest nights of my life.

For whatever reason there was a bit of a cock up with the care plan. It had been decided in King's Lodge that Geoff would need morning carers to help get him up, carers at lunchtime to put him back to bed and then evening carers to get him ready for bed, then an overnight carer as he woke a lot in the night and needed help being turned. There would also be physiotherapy, occupational therapy and psychotherapy which would take place either at home or at nearby clinics and surgeries. In short there would be a constant stream of human traffic pouring through Mum and Geoff's home for the foreseeable future. The first night, however, the overnight carer was not supplied.

We had set up Geoff's bedroom in the baby house for the time being as we were turning the old playroom into his bedroom and were in the process of turning Mum's study into a wet room so the entire downstairs could be usable for Geoff to live in. When they built a conservatory on the house, Sally was only three at the time and said it looked like a 'baby house', so the name stuck. It was decided that I would sleep in the living room which was next door to the baby house so that I could hear Geoff if he cried out and so that Mum could get a good night's sleep. The baby house had the best view in the house and looked out over the hills so he could look out across the valley, which he did enjoy.

After the carers put Geoff to bed, Mum and I set to the monster of a job of sorting out her study. It was full of boxes upon boxes of paperwork, photographs, 'just in case' yogurt pots and multiple other items. One of the brilliant and exhausting things about my wonderful mother is that each object (no matter how small) comes with a long and very descriptive story. Nothing is without purpose in her home. We spent a glorious few hours with Mum unearthing forgotten treasures and grasping them to her heart with tears of joy filling her eyes. Every 25 minutes or so Geoff would cry out for us and smack his watch against the bars of his bed. We would go through to him and try to help him get comfortable and then return to the job at hand. Mum was really exhausted that night but it was the first time I had seen her really happy in a long time, with memories of her past flooding into the room and sweeping her away for a moment. When she had gone to bed I stole some of the slides out of her collection, the ones that had made her laugh to tears with the plan to turn them into photographs for her to return to her at a later date to bring that happiness back.

We organised Mum's memories and vast piles of important papers as much as we could that night then took to bed – Mum upstairs in their room and me on the old sofa. Within minutes of drifting off I was woken by the watch-on-metal clang of Geoff wanting help. Bleary eyed I went in to help him. Confused, tired, frustrated and uncomfortable he wasn't sure what he wanted but he knew he was in pain and what he really wanted was Mum. The point of me being there, of there being a night carer, was so that Mum could have a break and sleep at night. I would help him turn, bring him a drink, alter the light, alter the radio, chat to him a bit until he said he was alright and then go back to the sofa for roughly 23 minutes before he would cry out for me again.

Each time he cried out for me he would firstly announce that he needed Mum and I would explain that she needed rest. This was not something he took well and would get very cross that she would get rest when he couldn't. Each time I would explain that it wasn't selfish of Mum to need rest and that she needed to be taken care of too and for the best way for her to be taken care of was for her to have rest at night so she could function properly throughout the day without falling down the stairs herself and then where would we be? His mood would then drastically drop to complete self-loathing and how wonderful she is and that she, of course, needs sleep and that it was selfish and terrible of him to even think of disturbing her. After this 20 minute conversation and gentle huffling and shuffling of him so he could find some comfort I would leave to go back to sleep and he would quietly utter; "So getting Mum now wouldn't be a good idea then?" And so this continued as such for the night until around 3am when he got extremely cross with me and really shouted at me to get Mum, which I did.

When Mum arrived we turned him together and she asked what it was he needed her for and he said he didn't really know and repeated to her about how uncomfortable he was and how unhappy he was about the whole situation and it was decided that there was nothing she could do and perhaps she should go back to bed. Perhaps we should all go back to bed. This cycle continued all through the night of me being woken every twenty three minutes (give or take) for twenty minutes (give or take) and waking Mum just twice during that time when he got really quite furious with me.

In the morning I reminded myself that I wanted children and that having a newborn would be like this. Since then I have had a newborn and it was not like that. That was much, much worse. Aside from anything, it is much harder to fling a six foot disabled parent over your shoulder and walk about the house singing Otis Redding until they fall asleep.

Fortunately there was just the one night where there weren't any carers and that was, for a while anyway, the worst night he had.

In time for his discharge, all the gubbins had been delivered and Geoff had a very snazzy hospital bed and reclining chair which, very slowly, moved him to standing, put him in the air, moved him to the left, lay him back down again etc. New plugs were being installed about the house for all the various different types of stand aids; we now had our very own Big Purple People Eater. Secret coded boxes were put outside the house so that carers could get in and get their own keys to let themselves in so we didn't have to, although perhaps a revolving door would have suited better.

The routine was set:

- **8:00am** – Two carers arrive to get Geoff up, wash him and put him into his wheelchair.
- **9:00am** til **12:00pm** – Geoff would have breakfast in the kitchen with Mum and she and someone else would help him get from wheelchair to chair with aid of Big Purple People Eater or Geoff would be picked up by Mark to go to various therapy sessions.
- **12:00pm** – Two carers come and put Geoff to bed for afternoon doze.
- **2:00pm** til **7:00pm** – Mum and someone would help Geoff into chair to watch telly, chat to cats etc. We would eat dinner together and chat giving Geoff little stints on the Standing Aid (this was not named).
- **7:00pm** – Two carers come to wash Geoff and put to bed.
- **9:00pm** – Night carer arrived until morning.

This would alter as the time went on depending on his ability and therapy sessions. We had some regular carers and some new ones. Renovations to widen the doors and make the downstairs wheelchair friendly were in full swing, including turning the temporary outside ramp into a permanent one. Mum soon got used to her home not being her home anymore.

Geoff, after wanting to be home for so long, took to being home with some difficulty. What he wanted was to be home and walking and well; not home and 'a fucking cripple' as he so delicately put it. His fierce denial and hatred of his head injury stopped any rehabilitation in its tracks.

When you are put in this situation you have to be prepared that your privacy does not exist any more. For both Mum and Geoff such things as modesty were gradually flushed away. Due to Geoff's nightly fretting Mum's sleep pattern was thin so was often greeting carers in her dressing gown and glasses, something she was not keen to be seen in. It takes a strong person to still smile when stripped down to your most vulnerable core in every way possible. Geoff, a gentleman all his life and still at heart, was literally being stripped down and washed whilst on a commode by young women (some less than half his age) trying to remain polite and witty to fight off the humiliation he felt by everything that was happening to him several times a day.

The worst part of the scenario is that you really don't know who you are letting into your home. The majority of the carers were lovely, compassionate and understanding but some were not. Mum's money had started to go missing from the little places she had always hidden it about the house for emergencies. Geoff was at spoken to so badly to the point that he feared the carers coming in case it was that person. We discovered that pornography sites were being accessed whilst we were out of the house and Geoff was in the next room on Mum and Geoff's computers. It got to the point where Mum had to take everything to bed with her including her handbag, and the cables to the computer; she was too frightened to point fingers as we were entirely reliant on the care we were given. To change carers, although possible, took a long time and was difficult. It is the same with everything in life: there

are some very good people and a few bad eggs who will take advantage
where they can. Such is life I suppose; but to know that someone was
doing this in my parents' home was like a constant kick to the stomach.
Mum really struggled with trust and didn't know how to deal with it,
as she feared that accusing someone would lead to offending the good
carers and having the support taken away, as there really was no way
of knowing who could have done it in some situations. The front door
was constantly being opened and closed by different people who all had
access to the keys and the house. It is all about trust really and respect
and this was abused and it has left a mark on my mother to this day.

I do not want to put an entirely negative spin on this because,
like I said, the majority of the carers were just incredible. They were
kind and respectful and they had a brilliant sense of humour, which
is exactly what you need. Life is laughter and if you can grip on to
that in the worst scenarios then every situation is worth living. We are
stupendously grateful to the good carers and there were many. They
made Geoff's life easier and they supported Mum and would listen to
her when she clearly needed someone to talk to. This was not in their
job description but they understood that she needed that. Sometimes
she needed to cry and sometimes she wanted to throttle Geoff and they
understood that and they never judged her. We were truly blessed with
those people.

6.

When things were good for a while

SOMETHING amazing started to happen; Geoff started to get better. His depression lifted and he tried. He was able to talk about his depression in the past, and although he could not remember it, he would ask about it and listen when we explained how it was. He joked how he didn't trust doctors before and that he would refuse medication and now he was seeing a therapist regularly and would take any drugs that would help.

He went out to physiotherapy twice a week and he went out to Headway Derby twice. Headway is a charity that runs projects and workshops for people with head injuries. He was encouraged to do things for himself and he wrote projects on people he admired and presented them to the other people there. He wrote a diary and his life story at home. He would get himself ready in the mornings and wheel himself through to the kitchen to make his own breakfast (albeit slowly). He would go into respite at Waltham House which were special flats kitted out for people with disabilities so that Mum could go and stay with friends or go to her house in France (where she would spend most of her time in a state of blissful unconsciousness waking only for food and wine to be posted into her mouth). He would call people and chat and we would go out for lunches. He would read books and be happily left home alone for hours where he would mooch about and do things. He would call me and we would chat for ages about life and our worries like we used to do. He was Old Geoff again and it was just so wonderful.

It was about this time I met my future husband Dan. Most young men would not be delighted, at the start of a relationship, to learn that part of their new partner's life is to help care for their disabled parent. But he did not blink an eye. Dan would come with me and whilst I cooked Geoff meals, he would chat to him about football and music. Both devout Derby County supporters and musicians they always had plenty to talk about. This was my favourite time. I was very glad that Dan came into my life when he did because he got to meet Geoff as Geoff, with his real personality and that still means so much to me because Geoff was a splendid creature and to have known him as he was really did add something wonderful to your life which never leaves. To have known *good* him made you a better version of yourself.

Mum's sleep wasn't broken any more. Although she was still exhausted from helping to heave her tall husband about, he was no longer waking her throughout the night, and the level of care he needed had reduced to the point where no one was required to come in the middle of the day any more. This helped home feel more like home. The renovations were complete including the fancy new stone ramp outside with a small patio, or sacrificial ground as we called it, in the centre. The doors all being widened meant Geoff could slowly move from room to room without help and the wet room meant he could have a proper shower. We put up important pictures of his, so it was *his* bathroom and nothing about it seemed clinical or demeaning – it's still one of the poshest rooms in Mum's house to this day.

Mornings would be relaxing now as Mum would go downstairs and get into bed with him, lying top to tail as they drank their tea and put the world to rights. They would be joined by Calvin the beautiful but enormous cat and life seemed quite normal. Mum was able to talk about how their marriage had been and Geoff was able to, usually, come back with coherent and well thought-out responses.

Guests would pop in to spend time with Geoff and he would be able to join in with conversations and, usually, stabilise his mood accordingly. He did get extremely tired very easily and he had no control over his ability to eat. Gentleman to the core, Geoff had a big gripe about meal times. He felt it rude to start before a lady and he also felt it rude for a lady to be left to eat last.

Meal times were important to him and our family. It was always a wonderful combination of politeness and etiquette and beautiful lunacy. We would sit in our allocated positions, creatures of habits our places had been decided by a higher force and felt wrong if sat in differently and we would dine together (at the table, not in front of the telly) and converse about our day. Mum and Geoff always ate together in the evenings no matter how late he got in, she would wait, so they could always dine together.

We had a *poubelle du table* which would sit in the centre of the table every meal time. France was a place that coursed through our bloodstream so it would trickle into everyday life whenever it saw a chance. Whenever Mum made plum pudding, and I can't remember how it started, the plum pit game would spring into action. Our chests would puff out and our eyes would narrow and with our figurative competitive hats firmly squeezed upon our heads we would aim and try and spit the pit into the *poubelle*. The winner was the person who could get the most into the *poubelle*. The game grew with time and if we managed a round (each person at the table landing the pit successfully into the *poubelle* in succession) we would all stand up and do one celebratory lap around the table before sitting back down at the next seat along to really test our skills and trajectory. Despite not actually liking plum pudding, I always looked forward to the days it was baked and it became a rite of passage for any new friend or boyfriend that was brought to the dinner table. A very good way to 'separate the wheat from the chaff' as Mother would say; and she was right.

When Geoff had his accident one thing he was never able to control was his eating habits. He would 'hamster' his food and eat like a glutton and he *hated* this. Always the polite gentleman, he would now swoop upon a plate of food and ram it into his mouth, sometimes to the point of vomiting afterwards. He appeared to have lost control of his self control when it came to food, or ability to understand it. Due to his family's problems with cholesterol and high blood pressure he had been very careful with food so that he would not follow in the path of so many Casboults before him, but now he would eat like a feral child and as a result his tummy started to swell. This also bothered him during his lucid times. "I wish I could help it," he said.

Although it only lasted six months or so I am so glad we had that time with Geoff. Where Dan got to meet him properly and he was lucid enough to understand what had happened and express himself. Although the next part was the hardest, it was good to have seen Geoff one last time.

First week back home with his bed in the baby house, having a cuddle from Tundee the old cat.

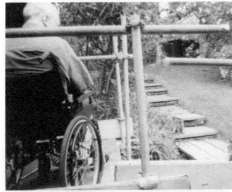

Sitting outside having a chat to Calvin the cat.

When he was able to read, having a relax in the garden with a bottle of water that mother practically forced down his as a preventative measure to try and stop the constant revisitations of urinary tract infections.

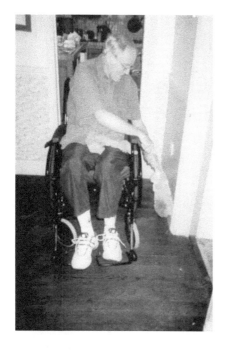

Mum putting Geoff to good use by getting him to do jobs around the house.

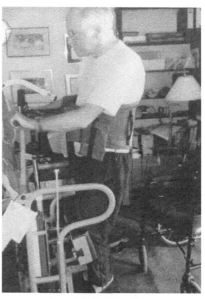

Geoff's Headway ID he carried with him in his little bag.

Geoff in the standing hoist at home.

 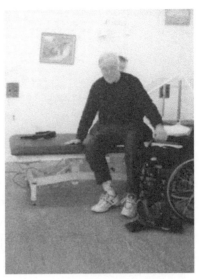

Geoff with the standing hoist at physio.

Geoff successfully transferring from chair to bed – these pictures showing how well he was starting to do.

Mum totally losing it when Geoff had armed himself with an umbrella hat, a broom and a small kitchen knife to save himself from the foliage which had started to get out of hand by the front door. A little glimpse into how things used to be.

7.

Weetos

═══════════

IN the Easter of 2011 Mum, Charlie, Maddie and I were in Mum's house in Brittany, France. This house she had bought when I was five before Sal was born. It is in a little fishing town called Erquy that Mum had come to since she was twelve with her parents and brother and sister, so the entire place means a great deal to our family and is like magic to us.

As children we would spend every school holiday in Mum's little house. Whilst we kids played at the beach or in the garden (depending on the season) Mum and Geoff would potter and paint. With it being empty throughout winter there was always little jobs that needed doing and they both really enjoyed spending their summer evenings sanding and repainting the shutters. There had always been a rule of no phone and no telly at the house so we children always read. We primarily read Bunty and Mandy annuals from the 60s and 70s; I am not entirely sure how this came about or how we accumulated so many of them but I have very fond memories of lying in bed totally engrossed in a story about a poor orphan girl who works for a mean mistress but then it turns out that they were accidentally switched at birth and the poor orphan girl then lives happily ever after (that sort of broad literary magic) whilst I could hear Mum and Geoff chatting in the garden and drinking wine.

These holidays were always very simple but very relaxing and enjoyable. We let the house out to friends and their friends, requesting everyone would write in 'The Red Book' (I suppose red books have a running theme in our family) to record their holiday antics. Reading other peoples adventures is always interesting and utterly hilarious and made us realise that we really are devout creatures of habit. In the 28 years we have been coming here we have not far veered from the routine, unless by great force (apocalyptic storms, stung by poisonous fish, favourite restaurant rudely changes hands to someone that objects to a sandy British family parking themselves at the same table daily to just eat *moules frites* etc) and that is how we like it. Even now, when taking my husband and son for the first time, he asking the question; "Ooh where shall we sit on the beach?" was met with a look of perplexed outrage from me and a; "Down by the ramp – *of course* – where else?". This place was/is our magical special place and the memories are a blur of amazing food, amazing weather, hours and hours of playing 'Three Bad Eggs' on the beach and as we got older; dancing to live bands on the port until the early hours and just constant ludicrous conversations and laughter.

After Geoff's accident he was not able to visit anymore. The house is perched at the top of a bank and is not wheelchair friendly. Crumbling steep steps to get to the garden, steps to get to the front door, outside steps and a beautiful spiral staircase inside. The possibility of even getting him to the country itself with the overnight ferry and long drive when he got uncomfortable and agitated after 30 minutes in the car was inconceivable, let alone getting him into the house itself when we got there, plus sorting out the 24 hour care package overseas… The prospect was improbable and this devastated Geoff. He would spend hours talking about ways in his head that it could be done but the issue there was that he was in denial about his head injury still so would say things like, "Well I could just walk up the steps", and we would have to gently explain and remind him that he simply could not walk.

Mum would come to Erquy for her respite and would often just sleep and Geoff would be very bitter towards Mum for the weeks leading up to her going as he felt it unfair. He would then relent and be incredibly apologetic and remorseful before she left. He would stay in

Waltham House when she went away and would have friends coming to visit, who were usually me or our very good friend Will Smith (not the *Independence Day* star). This time I was with Mum in Erquy too.

One day whilst we were all sat at the table my mobile rang. As a rule I don't answer on holiday due to the cost but it was Geoff, so I did. He was sobbing uncontrollably and saying how much he missed us, how much he wished he was there and how lonely he was. I can still remember the aching in my stomach listening to him cry. Up until that point he had been almost completely lucid so this was really out of character. After I finished speaking to him he then called Charlie and was the same with her. It was really out of character for him at the time but, with hindsight, I believe this was the beginning of the mania.

It was little things at first that followed, the occasional silly thing. He suddenly found the breakfast cereal Weetos utterly hilarious; shoulder shakingly, tear jerkingly hilarious. He would deliberately drop a Weeto on the floor whilst eating his breakfast and this would amuse him greatly. Every now and again he would peep under the table and see his Weeto sitting there and chuckle to himself. When the lady came to help Mum clean the house she knew not to tidy up his Weeto and he would be beside himself with giggles as she swept around it. We took a photo of a Weeto and set it as a screen saver on his phone and would listen to him losing it with laughter in his room and know he was just looking at his phone and it really made us all laugh together.

But then it started to get a bit weird.

His laughter became maniacal and he would laugh like this over the weirdest things, he also became furious and would roar in rage in an animalistic way. This was the scariest time for all of us. Sally started staying away from home more and more. Until this point she had remained living at home and would help out Mum with Geoff when she could. The whole accident had been a struggle for Sal and she had started distancing herself from Geoff from the point where he had started talking and had come out with bizarre things like thinking he was in Scotland and not realising his brother had died. This was a devastating blow to both of them. Geoff had always wanted to be a father and when Sally came along he just doted on her and the feeling was entirely mutual. They had a wonderful relationship and friendship. Sadly, Sally is very much like her father in that she deals with things by closing down and burying them. When he changed she closed down and drew back. Sometimes she was alright and the nights I would stay to help she and I would look after him together and then spend the evenings playing games and laughing, but when he changed she couldn't cope anymore and it was difficult and it was scary. It was made worse by the fact that Geoff adored Sally so fiercely that, when she came in the room he would instantly soften and stop screaming and swearing and would just say "Oh Sal – are you alright? How are you? I love you." She really struggled with the way he was so loving towards her but so nasty towards Mum and me.

Geoff started to get really aggressive towards Mum. I would call Mum most mornings on my walk into university where I was studying Fine Art, and it became impossible to talk to her on the phone. Geoff would become instantly furious and paranoid. The phone calls would go as such:

Mum: "Hello?"

Geoff: "Get off my fucking phone you cunt!"

Mum: "Please don't call me that, I am not a cunt."

Geoff: "That's my fucking phone, why have you taken it from me? Who are you talking to?"

Mum: "It is my phone and I am talking to Annie – would you like to speak to her?"

Geoff: *instantly softer voice* "Oh hello Annie, how are you? I was wondering why Mum has my phone – do you know?"

Me: "This is Mum's phone Geoff, I called her on it – please don't talk to my Mum like that, she doesn't deserve it. Please stop."

Geoff: "Oh yes of course, I am sorry, I am so sorry."

At which point Mum would take the phone back and he would instantly roar with pure hatred and start swearing at Mum again saying the most disgusting things and Mum would brightly say; "Perhaps we'll speak later?" It just became impossible to call Mum after that.

Friends' visits started to dwindle at this point too because he became strange. Fluctuating from maniacal laughter to roaring fury. Remebering that 'roar' of his still sends shivers down my spine to this day; it just sounded inhuman and not at all like the man who read me bedtime stories doing all the voices in silly accents. His eyes became wild again too; wide and darting and unrecognisable.

Mum went to Erquy again that summer for some very much needed respite and Dan and I went to Waltham House to cook him dinner. When we got there we found him sobbing; he knew we were coming as he had read it in his little red book. We asked him what was wrong and he simply said, "Oh Annie – I am so sorry." When I asked him why he replied, "I am sorry you were treated differently as a child, I am sorry you were treated differently to the others." This was not something I was expecting to hear and I had to swallow my tears like a Rubix Cube. "It's alright Geoff, it doesn't matter now, I know you are sorry – don't worry." I said. He seemed comforted for a moment and then looked down. He then looked up at me and sort of jumped with recognition; "Oh Annie – I am so sorry – I am so sorry you were treated differently as a child, it wasn't fair, I am so sorry." It was as though his brain had reset and he had forgotten the entire conversation three seconds earlier. "It doesn't matter Geoff, don't worry, I am fine, It was a difficult time for us all." – it didn't make a difference. It went round on a loop like that.

This was one of the most difficult times for me. I wasn't prepared for his apology as it was, but hearing it over and over made it difficult to breathe. This was clearly something that was haunting him; that had haunted him for some time. I took myself into the kitchen to get his dinner ready to busy myself. At this point I was so grateful for Dan.

He had not even been with me a year at that point and was used to seeing Geoff being relatively normal. He just calmly asked him about the football scores to distract him. This would only distract him for a moment as then he would see me in the kitchen and start crying and apologising again. At this point he admitted he had been looking at his life story that he had been writing on his laptop, and his diary and said he couldn't find me anywhere in it and asked Dan to help him; being computer savvy Dan happily helped. Geoff was right, he had not mentioned me once in his life story in his diary. Despite the fact I visited him everyday in hospital and had come to help care for him a couple of days a week since his accident nearly two years previous, he had not mentioned me once. This was hard to swallow; despite all I had done he had still treated me differently and 'cut me out'. This affected him badly and he began to repeatedly apologise and sob. At this point I couldn't stop myself from crying and left the flat to call Mum. My poor mum who just wanted a week's break was sitting on the beach listening to her daughter uncontrollably weep down the phone.

I had always known I was treated differently, his temper was always much shorter with me and I often felt like an irritant to all of my parents which had made me distance myself more. Whether it was in my head or not, I did pull myself away from the whole family by choice and ostracise myself as it felt easier, I suppose. This was not Geoff's fault and I didn't blame him. I know I had been a difficult child from a very young age, I suffered with continuous night terrors and was very withdrawn at school. I was also tiny and had very strange eating habits. I know I was a cause for concern for the whole family, which was one of the main reasons I just removed myself entirely, so it did not surprise me that I was absent from his writings about his life.

When I returned he had asked Dan to download 'Annie's Song' to his computer. This song had no sentimental value, we never listened to it as children and I didn't really know it only as people singing the first few lines at me occasionally. When I got his memory stick to write this book after he had died he had obsessively downloaded copies of 'Annie's Song', though I still wasn't mentioned in any of his writings.

After that visit, Waltham House said he would not be able to stay there again; he demanded too much care as his mental state was clearly deteriorating. Mum needed more help at home but I struggled to visit as much now because he would just obsess about apologising to me for my childhood. Dan would always make sure he came with me for support and I was so grateful. The baby monitor we had so he could call us became like a horrible radio station. We would be sat in the living room after Geoff had gone to bed and we would hear his crying and mutterings crackle through the monitor. I would just sit there and gently cry.

"Oooh… ooooh…. OOOOH!! *sobs* oooh… OOH GOD I HATE THIS!!!! I can't cope!! Oh… ooh OOOOH I can't cope with this all! Oh what I am going to do RAAAAAAAARRRRRGGGHH-HHHH!!!!! Oh GOD *cries, sobs and roars* Why can't I die? Why will no-one help me? I don't want to do this!! Aaaaahhhhhhh *sobs* What will I do?? Who will help me? *deep throated agonising wails and cries* Please help me! PLEASE!! Oh God I don't know what to do. PLEASE OH GOD I HATE IT! *gentle sobs leading gradually to guttural screams like someone discovering their entire family has died* RAAAAAAAAAARRGGHHH!!!"

I would go in at intervals and ask if there was anything I could do and he would just apologise to me then tell me he wanted to be dead. I would point out that I didn't want him to be dead and offered him something in the way of a drink or sandwich instead. He would decline and I would go into the next room again and cry whilst he continuing screaming in anguish. I don't know if he thought he was alone when he was talking like that or if he didn't have the ability to understand that we could hear him over the monitor; either way it will not be something that will leave me easily.

One evening I was alone with Geoff; it was a Wednesday as Mum always goes to choir on a Wednesday. They both used to go and Geoff had gone occasionally since his accident but was not longer able to but it was important that Mum had that break once a week. I was doing university work in the baby house whilst he was in the living room watching *Grand Designs*. He called for me to come through and said, "Annie, could you please go into the kitchen for me, you know that little blue box on top of the fridge? Could you possibly bring it for me?" "Do you mean your pill box Geoff? Why?" I replied. At this point his face contorted with anger and he spat back at me; "Because I want to DIE. Give me the fucking box of tablets so I can fucking KILL MYSELF – just let me die!" at this point his body sank down and he softened and said; "Please… just help me die." I stood there disbelieving that he had even said those words to me; that they were out there with me in the room just floating about. The idea that I would kill my stepdad and then go on living made me feel physically sick and completely furious at the same time. "No parent should ever ask their child to do this, no child should ever be put in this situation – ever." I responded with tears brimming in my eyes and then I left the room and sat in the baby house and let my body be consumed with angry sobs whilst Geoff roared like an animal telling me to "Fuck off!" and shaking his arms furiously. I didn't go back into the room for an hour, I could see him through the French windows so I knew he was safe. He eventually sagged down and wept in defeat and I breathed deeply and felt my stomach churn. I messaged a few friends requesting something that would make me laugh with no explanation. All of them dutifully replied without asking as to why. I wish I had kept them now; I remember they were deliciously offensive and just what I needed at that point in time.

Things just became much worse after that. Geoff became physically aggressive towards Mum. He never hit her, but he would grab her and not let go and he was strong. One day, whilst he was going ballistic at her for something like turning on the light, she faked a heart attack, theatrically grabbing her chest and tumbling to the floor where she lay still for a moment. "Oh no… I have killed her… What do I do? I have killed her!" he started to quickly mutter, at which point her eyes flickered open and she said in a groggy voice; "Oooh did I faint? I am sorry I became so overcome by all your shouting and I am so tired; you had better be a bit nicer to me as I don't think I could cope again."

That day when I arrived Mum ushered me into the kitchen and, with a mischeivious glint in her eye, said; "I might have done something impish…." With a smirk she continued; "I pretended to die to stop him from shouting at me… What?? It worked! He stopped shouting." That woman is not only a tower of strength, she is an evil genius.

Two excerpts taken from Geoff's diary with three months between them. He would go back into his diaries at later dates and delete paragraphs, change the size of the font etc because he had suddenly forgotten how to use it. In the end we typed and he dictated.

7.04.11

In the kitchen again waiting for Tris who is taking me down to our church for Millie's funeral. Quintessential. An old fashioned English Church and an old fashioned English lady.

Comparisons between a few months and his ability to write.

31.07.11

birthday anwiwl ,ei

Geoff in France 1997.

Our little house in France.

Mum, Geoff and Sal in France 1995.

*Mum and Geoff with a tiny baby Sally in 1989 with
a friend having dinner in France.*

Geoff in France in the late '80s.

"Jump like you're in Baywatch, Geoff" France 1996.

Mum and Geoff on the port in France 2006.

8.

The Old Lodge

IT was decided that Geoff was becoming too much for Mum to look after and Mum, who had remained defiant that he should stay at home, realised upon returning from holiday that he was worse when around her. This wasn't very nice for Mum but she knew it was not about her it was that she was his wife and he had become petulant and angry towards her like a child who didn't understand and it was worse for them both.

Geoff's mania was all over the place and his aggressive mood swings and bizarre laughter were difficult for us all. Sally avoided seeing him all together and I struggled through the visits when I did go home and we became more and more reliant on the help that was provided to us.

At this point Mum had hired a private nurse called Jo who was just amazing; she really 'got' Geoff. Kathy got married in Thorpe (for the second time so Geoff could walk her down the aisle) and this was the first time a lot of people had seen Geoff for years, if at all since his accident and he was not good. He was wild-eyed and shouting and many people were shocked. I pushed him down the aisle and Jo stood with us whilst Kathy got married to Rob. Geoff was unable to remain quiet and kept on shouting and sobbing. I caught looks of concern and fear from the guests at the wedding and felt anger inside me. Yes, he did look and sound strange now, but he wasn't always like this and it had been nearly three years since his accident. If people had come to visit him when he was good they would have seen that; but they hadn't. I had to remind myself that some people did find it difficult and I *had* to respect that. I didn't have to like it, though.

It mattered a great deal for Geoff to be there but I did not feel like it was Geoff there. It saddened me to see him like that because I know he *hated* being like that and being seen like that; it just wasn't Geoff anymore and it saddened me to have everyone looking at him the way that they did. That was Geoff's last 'public appearance' before his funeral a year and a half later.

Mum had been told about The Old Lodge and how it had experience caring for people with head injuries, so would understand his erratic mood swings and odd behaviour. The matron was fantastic. She reminded me of my old Geography teacher Mrs Shermer; enormously kind and compassionate but, despite her petite stature, you *definitely* would not mess with her. From the start Matron was an iron force who fought for Geoff's happiness and comfort until the end, she also had no problem with telling him off if he started getting shouty and rude towards Mum.

The Old Lodge was closer for us to get to Geoff but his mania had become really severe. During one visit we walked in the door and he was smiling wildly and his eyes were wide and when we said, "Hi Geoff, how are you? We have come to visit," he started to laugh. He laughed high and fast and started talking quickly as though we were hallucinations he found hysterical. I started to water his plants as I did when I always arrived and he started to narrate what we were doing, getting faster and faster, eyes wide, smile wide like the Cheshire Cat, the air spinning with insanity. It was too much for me, I couldn't breathe and he scared me. One of the lovely young carers came in and I said, through my heavy shame, that it was just too much for me today and I had to go despite only just arriving. She had kind eyes and said it was fine and started to chat to Geoff and laugh along with him as though he was telling a normal joke. We left with him beside himself with wild fast laughter and I walked as fast as I could without running gradually feeling hotter and sick then got into the car and cried great heaving breaths with genuine pain with each intake. That was horrible. I hate how insane and frightening he looked. He looked like my stepdad but possessed by something evil and I hated even more my inability to cope with him in that state and that I was not strong enough to do what that lovely carer had found so easy.

It was at that point I decided that I needed to have a focus for him and me to help us both and give me a good distraction when visiting him so I didn't break down again; it would be scary again and I would just have to man up and deal with it. At the time there was a project starting on my Uni course called 'Boundaries' using film photography – I decided to base it on Geoff and me and use his old camera. He had been really into photography and took beautiful photographs (when he actually found the time and inclination to do it). I had his old camera, which he had treasured and lived in its own little posh leather case. I decided that if I was going to do this I was going to do this honestly from both our perspectives and not sugarcoat or hide anything as it wouldn't work. I checked with Mum and throughout, when Geoff had moments of lucidity, I would explain what we were doing together and so he understood and agreed, he always said; "If it can help other people then yes." So it started. Instantly, this helped me cope better. With each visit I completed a diary entry and was completely honest, which has been helpful to read later on as you find you block out the bad bits, especially the bad thoughts that *you* had.

He continued to obsess and his speech would yo-yo between wild nonsensical whispers and sudden aggressive barks which would always make me jump and then leave me feeling both angry and nervous. It is hard to remember that these things are out of their control and there really isn't much of the person in there that you love. You have to split your brain to be hard and non reactive in order to cope with the situation as well as not letting them see a reaction and have the ability to then switch to normal and compassionate for when the lucidity switch clicks back on for them. You don't want them to feel hurt and confused when the fog clears and, through the clarity, they see someone they love hurt, crying or angry and they just want to help them and understand, you don't want to tell them it is a result of their behaviour that they can't remember or control as that mortifies them. You *must* learn ways to cope. To harden and soften without real warning but to find a way to deal with that yourself, away from them. I found screaming in an empty field in the middle of nowhere pretty good.

His room was faced a fence and some houses; the view was not something to write home about, but he would often comment about how beautiful it was. On a good day he would hear you as you walked down the corridor; the excitement of your arrival would set off his tremors and his arm would make a *shshf shshf shshf* noise which would get faster as you got closer, like a puppy's tail. As you entered the room his face would light up and he would greet you with a cheery "Hello! How are you?" and he really meant it. We would exchange pleasantries and then he would start to drift, mid sentence, and look dreamily out of the window and laugh and mutter to himself about how beautiful it was out there, despite the fact there was very little to look at all. We would talk and laugh and he would ask about everyone and repeat himself a few times. Occasionally, we would bring in either an iPod dock or a record player and his old records. He responded well to music since it was such a huge part of him. We even brought in his own drum sticks but they lay next to his bed untouched.

For his 65th birthday we had bought him a digital radio to live next to his bed and being someone who was very interested in good quality, he loved it. We brought it into The Old Lodge with him so that he could listen to Classic FM. On more than one occasion we would walk in to find him roaring with fury and Radio One blaring out after one the carers saw it as helpful to change the station whilst sorting his room. He wasn't very good at being assertive and asking them politely not to change his radio; instead he would scream; "AHHHHH TURN

THIS FUCKING RACKET OFF!!!" in our faces as we walked into his room. We decided that a polite note to the staff would suffice to solve this problem so we had; "Please do not change Geoff's radio station – he likes it on Classic FM only" (although he did sometimes fall out with Classic FM's incessant adverts, especially the 'Compare the Meerkat' one which – even I admit – being bed bound with that bouncing round my ears every 23 minutes is some kind of hell for most people). We also had other notes; "Please do not put the overhead light on, Geoff prefers the side lamp" and; "Please don't touch Geoff's possessions without asking". Understandably, he became quite irked when someone, anyone, looked through his things without asking, even if just to tidy them. Often we would get roared at for taking his glasses without asking, even though we had asked but he had forgotten and we had taken them to fix and clean.

One of his hallucinations was about a six-foot woman wearing giant slippers (well, a woman of that height must have pretty big feet) who would come into his room and touch all his postcards without asking. These were postcards with photographs of table tops, which he had saved for the man from Nestlé. We don't know if anyone *had* been in touching his photos, but we did know that he did not have a collection of postcards with pictures of table tops on them; we didn't see any…perhaps the chap from Nestlé came to pick them up? His hallucinations were a constant source of amusement for Mum and me; the small string quartet in his room, for example, so small, in fact, they were sat in the sink. He would look at you with honest perplexity when you asked; "And where is this string quartet exactly?" "There!" he would say with great earnest. "You mean *in the sink*?" we would ask, pointing at the tiny sink for the staff to wash their hands in the corner of the room. "YES!" he would strongly retort, followed by an exasperated eye roll as though we had asked him to explain where his feet were. We did sometimes giggle but never at him, we never made him feel silly for something he had said but we did sometimes giggle because it was funny.

Geoff's basic hygiene made a rapid decline. Even though he was always clean-shaven his teeth were not good. My Grandpa was a dentist and had made him a very expensive bridge for his mouth and that had broken leaving thin metal stumps where two of his teeth had been. Mum would often go at him with various dental equipment, reviving her dental nursing days. As a hard incentive to brush our teeth as children, when we complained, he would tell us the story of how he used to brush his toothbrush against one of the exposed bricks in the bathroom, he had got away with this for months until his father had caught him and was not happy. We would laugh, but then he would pull out his three false teeth and fling them into the bowl of the sink where they would spin and dance before clattering into the plug hole and peer up at us. The colour would drain from my face and I would brush furiously. It certainly worked; I only have one filling.

The damage to his brain had slowly made his body clench up and his left hand had become a tight fist. I would try to ease it open making him shout in pain so that I could massage his hand and cut his nails. The nails had become infected and soft and were peeling away from his hands, so I would have to delicately cut them down. They had started to smell because they were no longer exposed to the air and his right hand was starting to do the same starting with his little finger and working in. The skin was peeling away around his eyes and face where he had started to pick at it and he had bitten off a piece of his lip, by accident, we assume. It was deeply saddening to see a man who would spend a good hour making himself presentable; combing his hair with his tortoiseshell comb and shaving his face whilst whistling through his teeth now had no understanding of how to use a comb. His hair was wild like his eyes and his teeth were crumbling away. He was beginning to become unrecognisable as a human, let alone a gentleman.

His obsessions increased to the point that long dead plants had to stay in the room. I had bought him a real Christmas tree as we had the tradition of having a real tree in our family. Christmas was such a magical event with the usual injection of strange family tradition at home and the decorating of the tree was no exception. The decoration box was never jiggled or replaced and it took a lot for Mum to throw something away. Scraggly bits of tinsel 20cm long, with sparse sprouts of shiny paper looking as though it had lived the majority of its life on the streets were lovingly placed on the real tree, the apple bauble which had been gnawed on by a mouse in the attic so looked like it had an actual bite out of it balanced on the end of a branch and the hours spent by Geoff gently turning each of the coloured bulbs to find which one was out of the fairy lights before arranging it on the tree all with the old Christmas carols coming out of the stereo. Christmas morning we would walk down the stairs (after the agreed rising time of 7:00am despite Kathy and my valiant attempts to persuade otherwise) and the twinkling lights from the tree would reflect on the bulging stockings by the fire and the wave of lovely yuletidey smell would hit you as you opened the door to be greeted by the sooty foot prints, the remains of the carrot and the glass of sherry that had been licked clean – Father Christmas had been.

Despite me watering the little tree a few times a week it didn't want to live, nor did the other two plants that we had bought him; but he did not want them to go so we continued to water the dead plants. He still had his 'Weeto' phone in his little basket with his red book and his radio; now somewhat battered and rather sorry for itself, would be tucked in his bed with him. He knew where the pictures were on the walls and he would refer to them often, either in a fond memory or a furious babble depending on the mood he was in. One day we walked in and there was much excitement as one of the ceiling tiles had come down after a leak from a storm so he spoke fast and excitedly about 'the roof falling in' and said how a man had come in, put a ladder by the little sink and looked through the hole. After that the ceiling tile had a water mark on it and he would look up to it and smirk knowingly.

Guests really dwindled now. Will Smith remained a kind and reliable constant for him and there was an ongoing tally of scores in the back of his red book of the games of dominoes they had played. Matron asked us to come and see her one day after we had politely declined the opportunity for Geoff to go on the trip to Blackpool for the patients with the staff. We had worried that he wouldn't be alright. Matron was her usual self, kind and assertive and quietly said that this may be his last chance to see the sea. I felt very silly; these people looked after him amazingly every day and were giving him the chance to have a final holiday and we wouldn't have to do anything and it would be good for him. It turns out she was right; he didn't make it to the next holiday. We gifted him with a disposable camera so that he could capture everything and we returned to photos taken by the staff of him on the pier with the other patients and Matron. What occurred to me were two things: how ill and disabled Geoff looked and the genuine love and care that was pouring from Matron. We were lucky, in the worst of times we were very lucky. There was also a cheeky photo of Will smiling widely at the end of Geoff's bed, so he had taken a photograph himself.

One of the other residents died leaving a room with a view vacant. A new resident was already queuing to be taken in but she was blind so they felt it would be nicer to move Geoff to the room with the view. He was very rattled by this at first and his shivering obsessions started to rise: "there isn't a stain on the ceiling any more," he would say, peering up nervously, his wide eyes quivering from behind his long unkempt eyebrows. I had started to read to him a few months before he moved rooms as he had lost the ability to read himself. We decided between us to read the books that he had read to us as children, incorporating all the voices for various characters. It never occurred to us, as children, to wonder why each character in the book came from a different part of the planet; why the Mum was Irish, the dad Scottish and the uncle from Newcastle (not to mention the postman from Frankfurt), we just knew it made us laugh. Each visit I would read a few more chapters and

Geoff would laugh as he remembered what was about to happen or he would interrupt me to tell me of something that was making him feel a bit bothersome.

As his birthday neared I was discussing with him what he would like, I mentioned perhaps what he would have had if he were in Erquy: some moules and steak and he smacked his lips a little and said that would be nice, so I did it. I cooked fresh moules and fillet steak then wrapped everything with tin foil and we drove over. Accompanied by fine red wine and a triple chocolate cake we sat in the garden at Old Lodge with Mum and Sal celebrating his 69th year. It had not long been his and Mum's 24th wedding anniversary but they had decided to save all their celebrating for that for next year as it would be the big one. Sadly they did not make that. Usually I bought Geoff a card and a gift to give to Mum (for birthdays and Christmas too) and he would dictate what he wanted to say to her, I would write it then he would sign it. We did this with his diaries too and he would grimace at how his signature now looked; it made him ashamed. It still didn't occur to him that the head injury had caused this, that it wasn't him, it just made him feel embarrassed by what he couldn't do anymore.

He seemed more lucid more often when in that room. Perhaps that is just how I have chosen to remember him in there. A close friend of his died when he was in that room. He had cancer and it killed him quickly. We put the order of service up on his bedroom wall with the photos that were spreading about the place. He would tell us about him when we came in; "You have heard about Charlie Henniker dying haven't you? He was a lovely man". His genuine fondness for people was always something to admire. He would always enjoy a idiosyncrasy of a person that no one else would pick up; his compliments well thought-out and concise. It was a charm that I have not seen since; he really noticed people.

The last Christmas Day, Dan and I arrived after lunch. Mother had been there all day and was loudly remarking on how bearable he had been. She is never one for discretion and didn't see the point in not saying things about him in front of him. They were laughing and the light was warm. That year we had sent out our Christmas card of our cat TomTom frolicking in the snow and I had Photoshopped a fine Santa hat on his head. Sadly he had died suddenly a few days after we had posted them out. Mum had got us a little black cat soft toy to help us get over his passing and Geoff had taken a liking to him and had him tucked up on the pillow with him. Sally had dropped in too and Geoff had been… normal, for a change. The whole evening was nice; really, really nice. There were no roars or outbursts and all normal conversations and genuine laughter. We were heading to Suffolk to see my Dad the following day and so that was the last time we saw him before everything went wrong.

*Walking Kath down the aisle when he was
starting to really get bad*

*Having dinner at Kath's wedding sitting opposite his dear friend
Charlie who died just a few months before he did of cancer.*

*All of us at Kath's wedding. I don't like this photo. I don't
like how his face and eyes don't look like him anymore.
It was a really sad time.*

The first photo I took for the project we did together. He knew I was taking the photo but he still had this wild-eyed, frightened look. He had this look a lot at this time.

"What a beautiful camera, is it mine?"

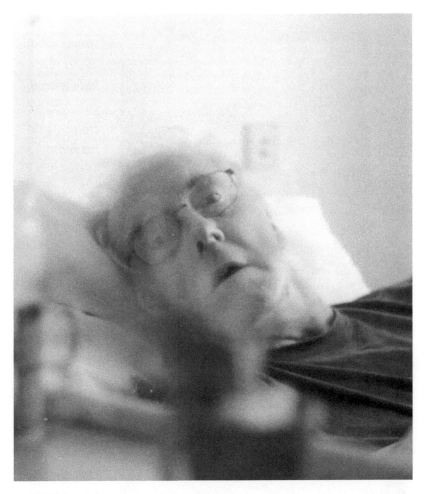

Initially I tried to take a photo of the snowdrops but then I focused on him at the last minute. When Ellen died he planted snowdrops on her grave, he then planted some in our garden so we always knew when we had flowers – so did she.

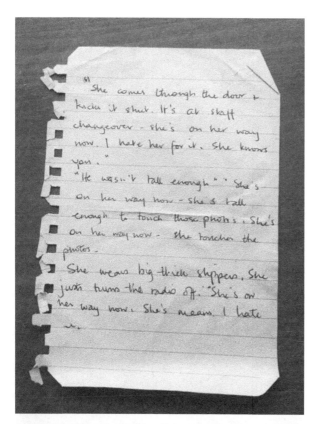

The conversation about the lady with the giant slippers coming into his room.

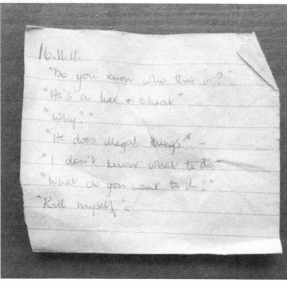

One of the usual cheery chats he had with Mum.

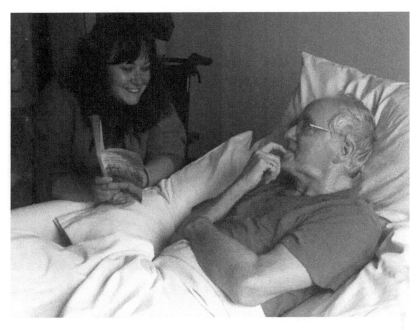

Me reading 'The Sheep Pig' to Geoff.

Magical and wonderful Matron with Geoff
on the trip to Blackpool.

Wonderful Will Smith – taken by Geoff.

Geoff's last birthday.

9.

Will I watch him die today?

IT is strange how things pan out. On the eve of the New Year in 2012, despite valiant attempts to party wildly into the night and run down the street in an inebriated state in our underpants; it didn't quite work out that way. We had invited our good friends Lauren and Leon over to stay and all of us felt increasingly tired and refused to budge from our jim jam clad state. After our Tudor-esque meal of meats and cheeses and a few glasses of wine we yawned in the beginning of 2013 and went to bed accompanied by the sound of other people's fireworks.

At around 7am the next morning I was woken by Mum ringing me; she was crying. Mum said that The Old Lodge had called and that Geoff was not responding and that they had decided to call an ambulance. For the first time in I don't know how long, Mum had spent New Year's Eve quite far away from home and was in Suffolk with Charlie and wasn't able to drive as she was so upset. Not wanting him to go alone to the hospital Dan and I got up immediately to drive over there to be with him. Whilst we were getting ready Sally called and was completely inconsolable. It is difficult to comfort someone when you don't know what you are saying is true. Was Geoff going to be alright? Would he die today? Was this really it? What if he was dead by the time I got there? I knew I just wanted to get out of the house and be there. Fortunately, due to the aforementioned night of feeble partying, we were fine to get up and go and Lauren and Leon were awake enough to understand what was happening so we left them to get up and go at their leisure and keep an eye on the cats. Not only did they do that; but upon our return home around midnight that same evening we discovered they had cleaned the entire house and made it all lovely for our return home. For me it is the little things like that which makes everything easier and really is part of the key ingredients in a wonderful friendship.

I don't remember the drive to The Old Lodge. I don't remember if we spoke; I imagined I probably prattled on asking incessant questions into Dan's ear without expecting or listening for a response. I do remember the weather was beautiful though. It was a really beautiful sunny day.

Ushered into the home by the concerned staff I walked down the long corridor leaving Dan to sign me in. I walked briskly; just choosing to ignore the expressions of recognition on the carers faces in my periphery. I have never been a fan of how people often speak to you during a sad situation. I find it too soft and false and unrealistic and feeling as concerned as I was then I would only have responded in an undeservedly sharp manner.

Walking into Room Six my eye panned past all the pictures and letters we had put up on the walls, stopped briefly on the paramedic sitting on the chair by the bed leafing calmly through notes and then finally resting on Geoff's face. His head was back and his neck strained. His eyes were bulging and staring towards the ceiling. His teeth and fists clenched and his whole body was vibrating. He was having a seizure. "So – your father has epilepsy then?" tumbled the cool remark from the paramedic. "No. No, my stepfather has never had epilepsy. He had a head injury and a stroke in 2008 and has been very poorly ever since. This is the first time he has had a fit. Do you think he is having another stroke?" at which point the paramedic stood up. "Oh. Oh, he's *not* epileptic? Oh, right. It might be a stroke. When the ambulance gets here we will be able to get him to the hospital and checked out as soon as possible."

Not really knowing what to do I went over to the bed side and took

Geoff's hand. As I said before, the brain damage had left Geoff with constantly clenched fists, but I was able to open it. He went through waves of fitting where he would rear his upper body up and his bulging eyes would focus on my face and he would let out a groan of anguish and then his body would relax and he would lie back and close his eyes with a painful sigh. I had never seen anyone having a fit before and now I was sat watching Geoff in a cycle of it happening every three minutes or so. It looked terrifying and utterly exhausting. I just spoke to him, the usual thing I speak to someone who I don't know if they're listening, stupid things. I spoke about how it was New Year's Day and how, on the night before, Dan and Leon had decided that they were going to streak naked through our village on the stroke of midnight but had bottled it almost immediately after both standing in our dining room in their pants and decided that perhaps putting their pyjamas back on and having some cheese was a wiser decision.

During this time the ambulance arrived and the two female paramedics asked for the lowdown on Geoff. Both were very warm and took time to listen. They were very impressed by the way we had scattered his life in pictures around the room and how attentive I was towards him, this baffled me as I honestly didn't think that I did a notable amount of care. I only visited him a couple of times a week, there were loads that visited their ill parents every day. Apparently most people just didn't visit at all. This thought baffled me even more but then I remembered my job working in a home for people with dementia and the rooms full of hollowed eyes; no one got a visitor. It was like a dumping ground for broken mothers, fathers, brothers and sisters.

It was decided that I would go with Geoff in the ambulance and Dan would follow behind in the car. The ambulance staff were chatty and kind and kept me completely abreast of what was happening with Geoff and what they were testing him for. He continued to seize throughout the entire journey whilst I apologised for the strong zest of alcohol emitting from my breath and assured them it was purely seasonal recreational breath rather than alcohol dependence.

Upon arriving into A and E at the Derby City Hospital (now The Royal) we were quickly shuttled into a large side room with big windows and the paramedics and I exchanged obligatory yuletide acknowledgments. As the door slowly shut the A and E out I became very aware of the solitude and the silence. There was Geoff in a stretcher bed in the centre of the room still going through these cycles of body clenching seizures followed by utter exhaustion and a clear urge to want to just sleep and me, sitting next to him, just looking at him. Dan was still parking the car and trying to find me so we were completely alone. What struck me was two things: imagining all those people in those homes who don't have family coming to visit them, one day ending up alone in a room like this on New Year's Day; perhaps somewhere else in this hospital right now. The other thought, as Geoff clenched my hand and stared at me with his eyes bulging and let out a cry of anguish, was; 'Am I going to watch him die today? Alone in this room with just the two of us, is he just going to die in pain and in front of me?'. I decided to message Kath and ask her that exact question. Her reply quickly buzzed in, "Yes. He could die in front of you now." Well… at least I knew and at least he wasn't alone.

Geoff and I were in that room alone for about an hour. Dan found us but then nipped out to call Mum (who was now, accompanied by Charlie, pelting down the A14 towards us) and Lauren and Leon to let them know that we probably wouldn't be coming home for a while and to ask if they could lounge about and keep an eye on the cats for a few hours. I read to Geoff and I sketched him in his quiet moments continuing on what Mum had started so that she could see what he was doing. After a time we were rolled through to a different room where he was examined and it was agreed by all that he had suffered a very large stroke and that was causing all of the seizures. He would be given an anti-seizure drug and be moved up to the stroke unit where he would stay until we were able to get him back to the care home.

Mum and Charlie arrived and we decided that we would all stay with him until he was in the stroke unit and we all knew what was happening and felt confident that he would be alright. So we set up camp around his bed. The medication had started to work and Geoff was asleep and just looked shattered. Mother, ever the creature of discretion had taken it upon herself to inform the staff who would be caring for Geoff of his recent exciting outbursts which had become more frequent since his condition had worsened of late. As the poor unsuspecting young doctor leaned in to hear what Mum was saying, Charlie, Dan and I all suddenly lurched forward to try and protect the Dr. as she said, "and he can hit you – like THAT!" and her paw, curled tight, jabbed viciously just a whisker away from her nose. "JENNIFER!" We all chorused just as she spun round, a cheeky grin starting to spread across her rosy face like a naughty little school girl – "I DIDN'T HIT HER!" she loudly defended before falling into her usual states of utter hysterics and tried to spit out the words, "I was just….. just… *pffffft* trying to *warn her* in case he woke up!" I am constantly thankful for my mother, but at times like that, especially so.

We all went home around 11pm after leaving Geoff rested in a ward feeling confident that he was going to be alright. I remember feeling so completely exhausted by the whole day. I had no idea that the weeks to follow would leave me an emotionally hollow husk. You often realise how resilient you are after times such as this.

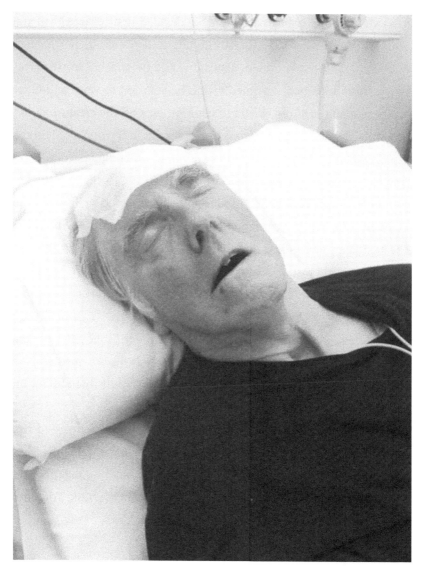

Geoff on New Year's Day 2013, trying to cool him down.

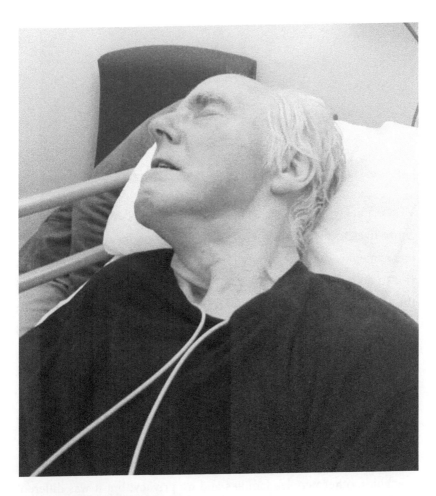

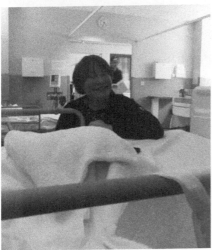

*Geoff on New Year's Day
2013 in pain.*

"What??!! I didn't hit her!!!"

10.

The Battle

====

VERY quickly we went straight back into 'hospital' mode; shifting our entire lives to fit around the allotted visiting hours and making sure that someone was there for each visit, or that you brought enough with you to do in the two hours break between visits. Sadly the Royal had the same rules as the old DRI when it came to the gap between visits; everything shuts so you have to find somewhere to lurk in the hospital to entertain yourself if you don't live close by.

I visited every day and decided to finish off *The Indian in the Cupboard*, a book he had read to us as children as I figured if Geoff could hear he would want me to continue reading to him rather than just harping on about my dull day or voicing how utterly terrifying this whole ordeal was for us all. We were back in the world of beeping machines, other people's families and no privacy; but it was different this time. With Geoff remaining unconscious this time and visibly dying, the lack of care and respect for him was evident. I know that doing the same monotonous job, day in, day out when you're exhausted can make you short tempered but surely when you are working with people; especially people at the end of their lives who are clearly not in a brilliant place; that is when you would take time to show the most respect.

It is not recognised how important the job of easing dying people through the last days of their lives is. This job is, primarily, done by the people who are never noticed or recognised. The hospital staff doing the night shifts and changing the pads of the incontinent patients so their dignity remains and addressing them by their names not even knowing if they can hear them. It is a humbling job to those of us who sit at a desk and earn five times more for selling advertising space on a calendar to large companies, and I think it should be acknowledged more. In the same breath it is a job that comes with huge responsibility and should not be done by an individual who does not approach it with the kindness and utmost respect which is imperative in the role. In the few weeks that Geoff was on that ward we were not witness to that respect and kindness very much at all and it caused anger and deep sadness to grow inside.

Mum and I took turns in visiting; she took the day shift and spent time chasing medical staff to see if we had a set date for taking him home. Trying to meet with specialists who were deciding whether or not the staff at the home were capable of tending to his NG tube then, in the next moment, trying to explain to staff that there was no point in bringing his slippers in as he had not been able to sit out in a chair for months and was in fact, quite clearly, dying. These frantic battles crammed into two hour periods had become a fixed part of our routine. Mum arranging for Geoff to come back to the home, gaining evidence from the home to prove they were capable, trying to find someone, ANYONE who she had spoken to before so that she didn't have to start her story from the beginning again. Exasperated that not one person had read our notes or even added to our notes and trying to chase down a doctor who would perhaps be able to give us the confirmation that he could go home; trying to find ONE member of the NG team who we could speak to face to face rather than through people and DESPERATELY trying to get all of this achieved before the weekend rolled by again as we knew that, come the weekend, most people didn't work apart from the nursing staff and healthcare assistants who were not permitted to make or confirm any decisions (but who, unfortunately, got the brunt of the distressed questions and frustrations). This constant battle would continue for the 2:00pm – 4:00pm visit and then

I would get a phone call from my poor withered Mum, pouring the information that I needed to check and confirm at the later visit before she drove home to get her work ready for the following morning.

I took the afternoon shift as it meant I could still go into university to try and keep up with my lectures. I would arrive for my 6:00pm – 8:00pm visit, with Dan to start with, then on my own. I miraculously passed my driving test on 11 January that year. I believe it was the sheer determination of knowing I NEEDED to be readily available for Mum and Geoff which pushed my anxiety aside and made me power through it (I also wore my Grandpa's socks for support, both ankle and moral; I sense they also gave me a hefty nudge in the right direction). I would spend the first 30 minutes taking on the duties of relaying my mother's questions and doing a general check over of Geoff. Echoing my mother's questions from earlier in the day: 'Why wasn't he wearing his own pyjamas when we had washed them for him?' 'Has there been any word from the doctor about a decision made from the nasal gastric team?' and always; 'Why hasn't he had a shave?' In my entire life I had never seen Geoff unshaven, ever. He was a gentleman of distinguished pride when it came to his appearance and he would take time and precision in polishing his shoes and keeping his hair neat with his tortoiseshell comb. He always wore the same aftershave and was never to be seen with a food stain down his front (quite the opposite of my wonderful Mum and I, who proudly fashion a blob of some dinner down 90% of the outfits we own). This was the first time in my life that I had seen Geoff with his hair unwashed and all over the place and he had a small scruffy white beard. These may seem like little things but the little things ALWAYS matter and especially in situations like this. These little things all built up the character which was my stepfather; the character which had been ebbing away gradually over the last four years, something which saddened us all deeply, including him. Little things like this, we did have control over and the responses when we asked were generally something along the lines of "I've only just come on shift so I don't know why no one has done it." or, "No one has the time, we are so busy." either completely avoiding responsibility or just making us feel guilty as they were busy. It is completely true: the staff are extremely busy in hospitals now; but to not shave a man, or wash his hair once in the time that he is there tiptoes into the area of neglect rather than being 'too busy'. Not one person said, 'I am sorry. Why don't we do it now?' I would have gladly helped; but all questions were met with the same exasperation and exhaustion experienced by the person asking the questions.

We seemed to be stuck. We just wanted Geoff to be treated with the respect he had carried himself with for his entire life and the staff just wanted to stop being the ones who had no power but were left to answer questions and carry the distress of the patients' families. Even more frustratingly, if we could just get him back to The Old Lodge then there would be people there who would be happy to wash and shave him, people who knew and loved him. If they would only sign the forms to let him go home.

After my ritual of unanswered questions I would straighten his hair as best as I could, give him any big news that had happened and then I would settle down to read to him. I would read loud enough so that he could hear but quiet enough not to disturb the other patients. I would sit huddled at the head of the bed loudly whispering the stories he told us as children and forgetting to do the voices. Sometimes he would open his eyes and look at me. His eyes fixed on mine with a look of deep sadness. I could see he hated what was happening and it was like he had given up. Sometimes he wouldn't open his eyes at all. He never moved his body at all, not even a finger. I had not seen him move since the day we bought him in and he had been having seizures. He was completely still. Still and sad.

When it was time to go home I would put my headphones in his ears and play him 'Local Hero' by Dire Straits. The song that, we discovered, was not only mine and Dan's song but also his and Mum's. I would play the length of the whole song to him so only he could hear it. Again his eyes would either be closed or they would be open and looking directly at me. I would sit in silence and look back. I never once cried in front of him. The whole time he was ill I did not cry in front of him.

These nights were dark and weighed on me heavily. When they first started Dan and I would drive home together and I would always ask to drive. I found driving an excellent way to steam out my brain and I would ask Dan to put on music to make me not sad. The first time I requested this he put on 'National Express' by The Divine Comedy, which was perfect. My fixed, furrowed brow and clenched jaw would ease and I would break into laughter and then tears and then laughter again. From that point on that song was played on the journey home and is still used for those same medicinal purposes to this very day.

We went round in this circle with nothing changing apart from the books. We finished *The Indian in the Cupboard,* then read *The Cat Who Came In From The Cold,* followed by *Tail Pieces* by the same author. I had just started on *Life of Pi* as I had been gifted the illustrated version for my 26th birthday and I thought that it would be nice for him to see the beautiful drawings for those little windows where he opened his eyes.

On the morning of 17th January 2013 I got a phone call from one of the hospital staff saying he was going home today and I asked them to let me know when so I could go with him. They promised to call and give me 30 minutes notice as I was with my great friend and business partner Rachel baking and relaxing at her house in Derby so I could be close by. At 1:30pm I was called to say his ambulance was coming at 2pm to collect him so I headed straight over to be with him.

What happened over the next eight hours I will not forget for my entire life. Upon arriving, I found Geoff in a separate room, sort of tucked away and he was awake. He had finally been washed and shaved but it was a shoddy job. Clearly parts of his beard had been missed and his hair left unbrushed. I noticed instantly that he was looking at me, I could see his eyes looking at me so I went to get a nurse, who got a doctor who just sighed and smiled and said that I was imagining it and that he was in a vegetative state and was now dying. I respected that he was a doctor but he just didn't seem to be dying. He didn't look great, don't get me wrong but he didn't look like he had done the day before. They informed me that they had stopped all medication for him but I also noticed there was no NG tube (something we had battled so hard to organise so he could go home) and no saline drip; there was nothing. Speaking to staff again they said they had taken him off everything as he was going back to the care home and that he had been off everything since the evening before. This struck me as a little odd that he was on nothing at all so I messaged Kath who said that his Liverpool Care Pathway should be in place so he should be having palliative care. When I spoke to the doctor about him not even having water he politely said; "He is dying – what is the point?". This small sentence still to this day bounces around the inside of my brain before tumbling into my stomach and spinning like a plate on the ground. What I should have said was this: "What is the point? WHAT IS THE POINT?! The *point* is that this man is a father, he is a good man, he is a funny man, he is an intelligent man. This man worked hard his entire life and watched people he loved die and cared for them, he carried us from the car after arriving home from driving us half way across Britain when he knew we were only pretending to be asleep, he helped clean up our sick and read us bedtime stories: the *point* is that this particular man should be at his home, clean and shaved and surrounded by people who care that he even exists whilst he slips away from us, not here being ignored." That is what I should have said and I will resent myself forever for not saying that. What I said was nothing. He then told me that I was imagining the recognition in his eyes because I didn't want to think he was dying and wanted to believe he was going to survive.

I stood there for a bit after the doctor had left doubting myself and thinking, really thinking about what he had said. Did I *want* Geoff to be getting better? Was I just trying to see something in his eyes to make myself feel better? I don't think I was. We had spent the last few weeks making the decision to let him die as comfortably as possible. I had signed forms with Mum the previous summer agreeing the 'Do Not Resuscitate' forms and had spent New Year's Day telling each doctor who saw him that was what we all, Geoff included, wanted. I didn't want him to live longer *like this*. He hated how he was before and now to be unable to speak but just to see and understand; I didn't want that at all. This wasn't something I was imagining to make myself feel better, this whole situation was making me feel pretty shit, actually. I felt sick and furious and a bit like a stupid little girl trying to convince someone that I was telling the truth and no one was believing me, like when I *was* a little girl. No. He was wrong. This was NOT me imagining things for me to feel more comforted. How could anything that was happening be of comfort to anyone? I felt livid. I felt sick and livid.

Geoff, who had been watching me the whole time, started to cry out in, what I can only imagine to be pain. I dashed to his side and ask him if he was alright. I called a nurse again and said he was in pain, can he not have anything? She said there was nothing he could have but she would ask. I didn't really know what to do with myself. I wasn't expecting this; time was ticking by and I had already been there for over an hour. I wasn't prepared for this. I didn't have books to read to him in my bag, food for myself, I hadn't eaten lunch because I had been preoccupied, I didn't even have any money as I was expecting to go with Geoff at 2pm and be at the home for 2:30pm where they offered you a cup of tea and a sandwich and chatted to you. I wasn't prepared for any of this.

I started to pace and think, walking around the bed with Geoff watching me. I decided to play him the song I played him every evening so far: 'Local Hero' (fortunately I always have music with me; music over sustenance every time) The second the song came on, Geoff started to cry; really sob. This took me by surprise as I had played this to him every night since New Year's Day and I had had no response at all and now this. Jumping up and trying to catch my breath I spoke to him clearly. "Geoff – can you understand me? Do you understand what is happening? We have agreed to let you die and not keep you alive with a tube. Do you understand? Is that what you want? We are here and we love you." He looked at me and tried to speak but he couldn't form words, he just howled and made burbling sounds but he was trying to speak and could not stop crying. I don't know what he was trying to say but deep down I think I know. I think that, despite his desperate pleas for us to kill him and let him die over the past few years, I don't think he wanted to die yet. I think he was more alive then we were told he was, and I don't think he wanted to die. Forever, and I mean forever, I will be haunted by the knowledge that Geoff was asking me to help him and I couldn't do anything – I *didn't* push harder to help him.

I asked if I could give him water on a little sponge and was told I could 'do what I wanted'. When I tried this he sucked on the sponge, clearly very thirsty, but was then coughing as he was lying flat. I didn't know if I could move him and there was no one to help me. I tried to give him a sip of water again and again he was desperately trying to get more water and started choking and coughing again. I didn't know what to do, I was out of my depth, I didn't know if I was making it worse or not. I knew he was thirsty but I couldn't stop him from choking and no one would help me. I sat on the floor next to his bed and started to cry. I told him I was sorry and that I knew he was thirsty but I didn't know how to help him and he put his head back on the pillow and sort of shouted and then was still and crying. I can't express how guilty and hideous I felt. I felt powerless and useless and shit – really, really shit.

Despite me repeatedly asking for more staff to help, no one came. Dan arrived after work around 5:30pm and found me on the floor by his bed crying and Geoff in his bed howling; both for the same reason I think. I am so relieved Dan was able to be there with me. I am so glad he saw and heard Geoff too. Kathy also heard over the phone; she had recently given birth to my nephew Wilbur and he was joining in with the crying over the phone. Kath said that those noises were not normal for someone who is as the staff said Geoff was and that he needed to be reassessed. I felt so glad I was not alone and that other people witnessed what was happening because it is hard not to doubt yourself when you are being told that you are imagining everything that is happening. Especially when it is medical staff who almost laugh it off.

The battle continued on as snow started to fall and it became dark outside. Eventually, at 10:30pm there was an ambulance free to take Geoff back to the Old Lodge. I followed in my little yellow car – I was so glad I had passed my driving test when I did and driving in a blizzard late at night through country roads six days after passing your test is certainly good for getting you into the zone.

Upon arriving back I was greeted by the night nurse who knew Geoff, although I had not met her before she knew of me and she really did know Geoff and that instantly made me breathe again. We got him into bed and I cried on her with exhaustion and relief and deep sadness. She was not happy that he had been brought back without any pain relief but there was nothing more we could do.

I sat there in the darkness with Geoff for a bit. It was now almost 11.30pm and I knew I had to drive home, Dan was already there and had gone ahead to light the fire and prepare food etc. Geoff was visibly more relaxed for being in his own room and the nurse had put on his radio on Classic FM as he liked. Little things showing little amounts of care for him make all the difference, always the little things.

I sat there looking at Geoff and Geoff looking back at me for about twenty minutes I think. Not long. I just kept on saying I was sorry that I hadn't been able to get him back quicker and that now he could be more at home. We looked at each other in the dark and sadness was wrapped around us as the snow fell heavily behind me out of the window in his room.

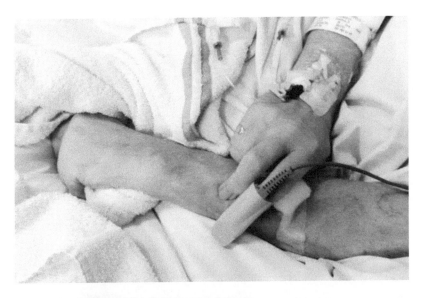

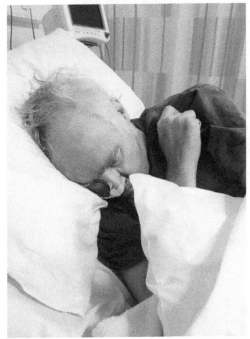

Geoff's hands, motionless, bruised and tangled with wires. Ward 410.

Geoff, unresponsive, in ward 410.

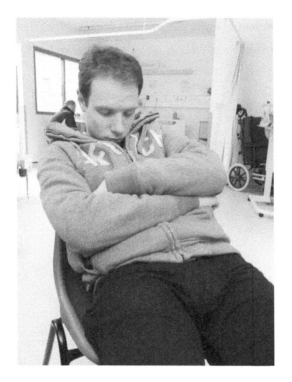

Dan catching a nap whilst I read to Geoff. Ward 410.

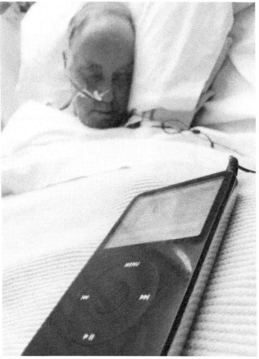

Nightly routine of playing 'Local Hero' by Dire Straits to Geoff who remained unresponsive. Ward 410.

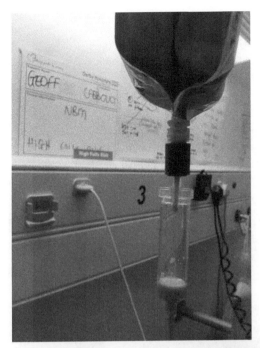

The NG drip which was the argued reason why Geoff couldn't go home. The 'high falls risk' warning for a man who couldn't even lift his own finger. Ward 410.

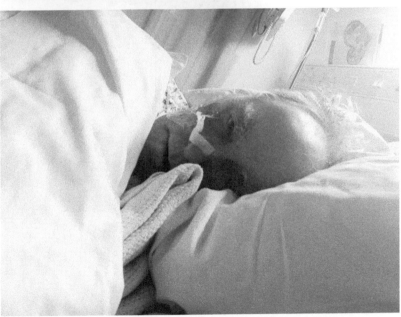

The horrible look he would give me on the occasions he opened his eyes. The look of deep sadness. Ward 410.

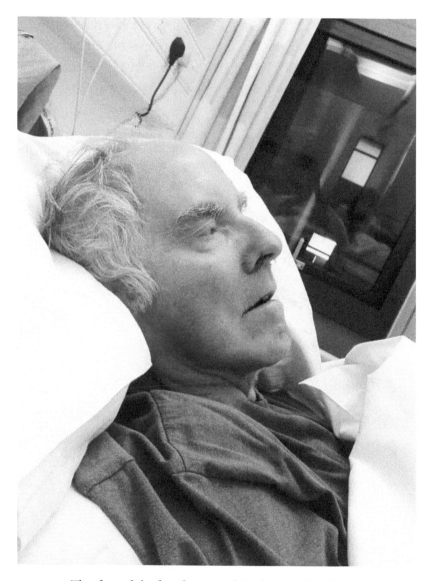

The day of the battle to get him home. Ward 410.

11.

The Final Days

WHEN I arrived at The Old Lodge the following afternoon I saw Matron at her desk in her office talking sharply to someone on the other end of the phone. She ushered me in and it was clear she was talking to the hospital about Geoff.

"I do not believe this man to be end of life. We need to have the doctors permission to give him a saline drip now. I know this man and he is responsive, he is not end of life." she said with angry passion. After putting the phone down she burst into tears and then hugged me. I cried too. I seemed to be on the brink of tears all the time. We walked arm in arm to Geoff's room and he was sleeping, she said that she agreed completely with me and that he had been trying to talk to her too but that the hospital had not sent any signed information over so we were not allowed to give him water. I still gave him sips of water from a spoon because I just felt I had to, but the staff were not allowed to do anything and you could see the clear frustration and concern in their eyes.

Geoff was washed, cleanly shaven and in his own clothes. He was back in his home and he was visibly more relaxed. I continued to read him *Life of Pi*, holding up the book for him to see the large and beautiful illustrations. He did open his eyes but they rolled in his head a bit, he just seemed so very tired now.

Mum came with Will and he tried to speak to them too. Sally had decided that she didn't want to see him after he had been admitted to hospital again. Mum told him that we all loved him and he cried and she knew I was telling the truth. She and Will took it in turns to go out into the corridor and cry. I went every day, reading and taking photos of the room and him and sketching. I felt it was important to continue our project to the end and it was what I had always done. I sat in the room peacefully just sitting still and listening to the quiet and looking out of the window and everything around his room. The photos on the wall stuck up by us, the drawings, the orders of service from the funerals of his friends who had died whilst he had been in there, post-cards from friends and from us, the little – long dead – Christmas tree that he wouldn't let us take down. He had been here a long time and it had been a real home to him. The staff had been amazing and they just cared for the people they looked after and it showed. I was so happy we had found this place.

Geoff's view was lovely since his room had changed and whenever he opened his eyes he could look through his window to the garden and the fields behind. The garden where we had celebrated his final birthday. As I said, I had made a real effort for that birthday and I don't know why I did as it was his 69th so nothing special. It would have been what he would have eaten had he have been in Erquy so I tried to rep-licate that for him and I was so glad I had done that.

On Tuesday 22nd January he was finally given a saline drip – by this point he had been without proper water apart from spoonfuls for a week. His decline was rapid. We never had any illusion that he would live forever but we had hoped that the time he had left would not have been as rapid and undignified.

On Friday 25th January I came in to see him knowing that Char-lie was already there. Despite being with him the evening before, he looked very different; he looked terrifying. He looked dead. There was this horrible rasping and gurgling noise coming from his throat, he looked like a zombie. It was as though he was already dead but some-one was pumping his chest with a dinghy pump causing that *whoosh* of air each time and making his body lurch. My mind went back to the beach in Erquy and Geoff blowing up the dinghy for us with the foot pump after Charlie had fainted trying to do it herself. The sun shining and all of us lazing around by the sea…

'Lark Ascending' was on the radio and Charlie was crying softly and holding his hand. Upon seeing him, I suddenly couldn't breathe. He had changed so quickly in such a short amount of time. I went to Matron's office but she wasn't in; the lovely carer who had dealt with Geoff's mania so kindly was there and she gave me a very heartfelt but very awkward hug. As lovely as this lady was, she was not a hugger. I said that I felt like he had stepped up his game a bit and was really on the way out (I can remember using these very undignified words as I couldn't catch my breath or even think of how to say it properly) she said he was dying and it was sad and walked with me back to his room but upon walking in took a step back and then said that yes he had progressed further and she would go and call the doctor about any medication he may need. Kathy had told me on the phone about the strange sounds that come from people when they are dying and that they can be a bit scary so I went into the car park to call her and prepare myself. I explained what he was like and she responded that the noises I was hearing were the 'death rattle'. She said that he would not be feeling anything now and from here on it is much worse for the people with him rather than him, his body is just coming to an end.

After five minutes of crying, composing myself and crying again, I took some sharp deep breaths and went back in. Charlie was just leaving to go to Mum's and I wanted to stay with him, but I had promised to pick up Sally and take her to Mum's too so I couldn't. So I went back in with him for a bit and cried. I decided not to take a photo of him like this as he just didn't look like him. His body, which had spent the last month tense and screwed up was now relaxed. He was propped up, with his arms and hands out flat on a cushion, and with each rattling breath his body would deflate and then pop back up like an old wooden Push Puppet. His head seemed bigger as his eyes had started to really sink into his skull and the skin around them had darkened. His mouth was locked open and his lips, although already thin, were receding and his teeth seemed bigger somehow. He looked like a corpse marionette from an old stop-motion film. Geoff had already gone, his soul and essence were gone and his poor old battered body was just winding down.

I left, with the gentle sound of his radio playing Classic FM and his gurgling raspy breaths echoing in my ears.

We spent the evening at Mum's talking about the funeral plans and what mattered to everyone. An odd feeling; planning the funeral for someone who was still alive but who you knew would die in a matter of hours. It mattered to me that he was buried in one of his suits as it always mattered to him that he was dressed smartly, something that he had lost control over in the past six years. Mum said that wasn't important and that a death shroud would be absolutely fine. Charlie agreed with Mum, Sally didn't have any strong feelings about it. This *did* matter to me, it still does. He was buried in a death shroud.

We spoke about who would want what of Geoff's that mattered. We agreed that we wanted Will to have one of his important clocks, there was nothing of any real monetary value; all sentimental. I asked for Uncle Michael's boat. This boat was never completed as Uncle Michael had deemed it 'not good enough'. It was beautifully crafted with each tiny nail and wooden board hand made, it was always something I wanted to play with as a child and was never allowed. It would stand on top of the tallest bookshelf and I would stand at the bottom looking up longingly. Now it stands on the tallest shelf in my home office so that no one can touch it.

That night was the worst snowfall in years, as though someone had flopped an ocean's worth of snow onto the Midlands. We had been forced to abandon our car and walk home the night before. At 5:30am on Saturday 26th January we were called by the lovely nurse who had greeted me when he returned from the hospital and told me I had to come now to say goodbye; but we were trapped by the snow. This saddened me deeply; Geoff was so frightened of being alone and without us and now he was dying without us which was what I really did not want. The lovely nurse stayed with him to the end and then she closed his bedroom door and left his radio playing for him until the undertakers were able to pick him up, which wasn't until 2pm that afternoon so perhaps it was better I wasn't there as I would have been snowed in away from home without the rest of my family. Maybe it happened for a reason.

We got up early and went sledging in the deep snow. I felt him walking alongside us, not in his wheelchair but walking and I knew he was alright. We threw ourselves into the snowdrifts and pelted down the hills near our home. That is definitely what he would have wanted.

Once back at the Old Lodge I would photograph his room to keep myself occupied, to finish the project we started and to remember how it was.

One of the many notes we had around the room to keep Geoff's stress levels down.

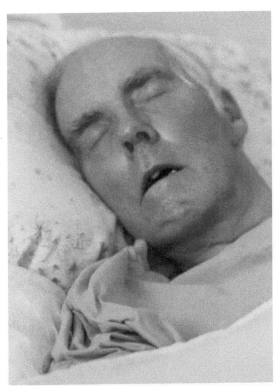

Geoff, having been starved of water, barely opened his eyes now.

The photo I had taken of him and Mum in France in 1998 when he looked really happy. He loved that photo. It is now up in my kitchen.

*Reading Life of Pi to him. He died before I finished
and the bookmark is left on that page.*

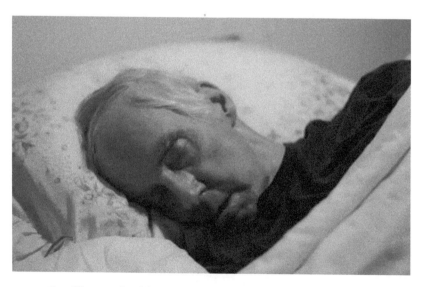

*Geoff's eyes had become noticeably darker and sunken.
This was the last photo ever taken of Geoff.*

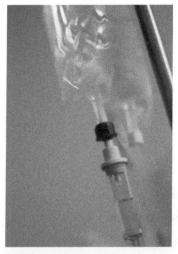

The long awaited saline drip that he got after five days.

He died listening to his beloved radio. They left his body in the room with it still playing classical music.

Geoff in 1988 looking across the snowy roughs. It snowed just like this on the morning of his death.

12.

Sally

WHEN I started to write this book, I offered Sally a chance to put her perspective forward as someone who had really struggled. When she replied I was so proud of her courage to be totally honest about everything; not many people would talk about this so publicly and doing so will help others in the same situation can understand.

Dad

What I liked about him before his accident
- His generosity.
- His understanding.
- His love of music.
- His morals, how much good manners meant to him and how much it meant to him for us to learn them.
- How he made an ordinary family meal a special occasion.
- His sense of humour.
- His mannerisms – drumming on the table, singing songs that include words that you have just said in a sentence, reactions to a riff or a note that he loved in a song in the background.
- How romantic he was with Mum.
- How he let me be me.

What I liked about him after his accident

- How he wanted to keep his appearance and dignity.
- He maintained his sense of humour.
- His overwhelming love and gratitude to friends, family and carers who helped/visited him.
- His moments of clarity – when he would remember something that happened long ago in a lot of detail. One of my favourite moments was in ICU when he was still heavily unconscious, but when the nurse asked him to stick out his tongue, he did it quickly, like he used to, when he was being cheeky (or "impish"). It felt like the Dad that I remember popped in just for a little bit.

What I didn't like about him before his accident

- How stubborn he was.
- How he protected me from how he really felt. I think he was trying to help, but since everything has happened and now I know that he was unhappy for a long time, I wish that he didn't have to pretend to me that he was okay.

What I didn't like about him after his accident

- How frightened and confused he looked.
- How he sobbed – I found it worse when he did it as I came into the room.
- His angry shouting and screaming.
- His posture, how frail he looked.
- Knowing that he was suffering and unhappy with his state.
- How he said things that didn't make sense (although there were some funny times!).
- To me, he was a completely different person.

Why I struggled to visit him

When Dad was first admitted, I would visit him almost every day for as long as I could, even if he was sleeping the whole time. It upset me a lot sometimes, but it didn't stop me from visiting. This started to change when he was in the Derby Royal hospital and I think it had something to do with the fact that the painkillers that he was on made him do and say really strange things. Sometimes he would say stuff that was quite funny and then during one visit (I can't remember what he said) he shocked me. Mum was there at the time and later told me that she could actually see me backing away from him; I can't remember doing this at all. Even though I had been there for five minutes, I really felt like I couldn't be there with him. It's hard to explain, but my brain just couldn't make sense of what was happening and I just wanted to escape from it really. I still visited from time to time after that, but not nearly as often.

After neuro rehab, when he eventually came back home, he was the best he had ever been since his accident and it felt easy to be around him. I enjoyed helping him with the physio and getting him in and out of his hoist. I was still sad about what happened, however I really felt like I could cope because there was progression.

He was ill over a winter where we had a lot of heavy weather and his health began to slowly deteriorate. It was little things at first, his angry bursts or how he'd keep talking about how 'doomed' he was. I led a quiet childhood and was never used to confrontation or behaviour like this, especially from Dad, so I found this hard to see and listen to. I would just shut myself in my room. The angry bursts got worse and he sometimes became manic. When he was like this, my fear or shock of his behaviour turned to anger. I couldn't register that he wasn't able to control how he felt, so I was angry at him for screaming at carers and at Mum, because that wasn't him. I was also angry because whenever I came into the room, he wouldn't scream or shout at me. It sounds a terrible thing to say, but at the time, it made me think that his behaviour was superficial because of this and avoidable for Mum – why did she have to deal with that but not me?

When times were at the worst at home, I hated him being there. I loved him, but I hated how he was behaving and how angry he was about his situation. I felt that he needed to be somewhere else, where a professional could look after him and suit his needs. Saying that, the idea of him being somewhere like a nursing home absolutely terrified me. I've been on work placement at some care homes that were not to the best standard and to picture the man I knew and loved being in one like that made me feel sick. Still, I felt like our house wasn't the best for him. My Mum is really strong and could deal with his outbursts, but I couldn't. I found myself staying at friends' houses, I suppose for a break from it all.

The time period where I really struggled to visit him was eventually when he was taken to a nursing home. I was dreading it, but I bit the bullet and went to see him when Mum was there for support. When I saw him, I burst into tears almost instantly. In my eyes, my worst possible fear of how he would be, had come true. He was talking to me quite calmly and didn't notice my crying and I tried to talk back to him but I couldn't, I just sobbed and sobbed. I don't know what went through my mind, but I think realisation hit me and I was despairing. I left five minutes later.

After that, I rarely saw him, perhaps once a month and my visits were very short. I did this for a couple of different reasons. One was because I couldn't cope with the truth that he was getting worse and one was because of his reaction when he sometimes saw me. I can't put into words the smile on his face when I would come in and the way his face would screw up and he would sob and wail. I felt guilty for making him feel like this, I didn't want to bring him down or remind him of what he didn't have any more. He would apologise to me repeatedly, for letting me down and it felt awful. It wasn't true of course, but I felt that I was making him feel this way and it wasn't fair on him. I stopped visiting him on my own and when I did see him, it was always with someone there, it seemed to take the edge off his reactions. I often imagined him lonely and frightened in his room and it broke my heart, but I couldn't bring myself to see him.

The last time I ever saw him, I had a nice calm time with him and Mum. He liked the coat that I was wearing and liked to stroke the sleeves. I was beginning to feel overwhelmed and so I said that I was going to leave. I gave him a kiss on the cheek and said; "love you lots" and he said; " I love you too". He was quite good that night and I felt that it was 'Old Dad' talking.

On the morning of New Year's Day, I was told that he had a severe stroke and was unresponsive. I remember that moment still, I was in my room and I broke down and couldn't move. I called Annie to find out what was happening, she reassured me, but I couldn't say anything because I was just terrified. I'd known that he didn't have the best quality of life, but I was still so shocked to hear the news – it felt like I had been punched in the stomach. I stayed in my room all day, just numb. I hate to say it, but I can't remember considering visiting him in hospital that day. I don't know why, maybe I was trying to take it all in.

I can't really remember the next month after. I was in what I call 'autopilot' and my brain felt like it had been in a washing machine. Mum and Annie told me that when they saw him, he looked very different and was really in a bad way. This frightened me and for me, it was just easier to cope with things by not seeing him. I had this lovely memory of the last time I saw him and in a way, I didn't want to taint it. Some people never get to say what I did to someone they love before they die and I felt really lucky. Especially for the fact that when I spoke to him, he seemed to be the man I remembered and not the man he had been for the past three years. It felt really special. I spoke to some friends for advice and they all told me to go and see him, that it would help him and that I would regret it if I didn't. I knew they were right, but I just couldn't see myself doing it. I saw a wall between me and him that I couldn't get through, I don't know why. I did finally string up the courage to visit him in hospital and when I arrived, his bed wasn't there, I think he was having an X-ray. I'm not a person of faith, but I took this as a sign from him. Perhaps I was reaching for an excuse, I don't know, but at the time that was how I felt. After that, I started to reassure myself of my coping mechanism because I knew that I had the chance to tell him that I loved him when he knew what was going on – I heard that it was very unlikely that he knew what was happening around him at that time.

When I heard that he died, I was very calm. I was deeply upset but I felt peace for him. This was heightened by the fact that there was a set of tyre tracks which formed the shape of two hearts linked together in the snow just in front of my bedroom window. I felt like my brain connected with him and I said goodbye to him aloud on my own in the very early hours of the morning.

Looking back now, I realise that my coping mechanism was just to escape from the whole situation. Seeing a parent in trouble when you have barely hit your twenties is difficult and it is much easier to just not think about it then to deal with it head-on. I loved him so much and I truly, truly miss him. If I could go back in time, I wished that I spent more time with him towards the end and focused more on what was going on, rather than how I felt – how I could have been there for him, how great his nursing home was etc. My method of coping seems selfish to me now and I hate that it does. Nonetheless I still don't regret my last time with him and I cherish it.

I am so thankful for my family's strength and for how they supported my Dad through the really difficult times. I am also so thankful for the fact that I was never pressurised to see him if I wasn't ready, because they were very understanding.

I think it is normal to feel frustration and fear during times like these, but now I know that I could have done more and I sincerely wish that I had.

Sally and Geoff in France 1992.

Sally and Geoff in France 1997.

Sally and Geoff at home 1993.

*Sally with Geoff and Kathy and me in
1999 in the garden at home.*

13.

The Funeral

THE world stopping snowstorm had put a little spanner in our spokes. Geoff was snowed in at the Derby morgue so I couldn't go and see him as I had hoped to. We went straight into organising mode for the funeral and wake, deciding little things, like it was best to have a caterer so we didn't have to think about the food; planning the best way to do it, the way he would have wanted, as well as us. I knew I wanted to talk about Geoff. I had noticed that, as soon as it was common knowledge that Geoff was dying, people started to relax and reminisce before he had even died; glossing over his time after his accident and it mattered to me to talk about that time because he hadn't died in 2008, he had died yesterday.

It felt as though many people just felt relief it was over and they could now mourn him, rather than occasionally remember he was still alive but not the person they had known and either have a short and uncomfortable visit or not visit at all. I wanted to properly remember Geoff for everything, not just the man he was before the head injury.

Mother and I came to the Old Lodge to clear out his room. Signing in at the corridor that was so familiar to us now we were greeted by genuine hugs and well wishes from the staff who had come to know us all so well over the past two years. Mum was very short and sharp with me and I let her be, I couldn't even imagine what had been going through her mind at the time and how she would be feeling but I knew that, much like me, organising and being busy helped so I let her get on with it. We took all the photos and pictures down off the wall and decided that we had to be ruthless and throw away the little dead Christmas tree that had mattered so much to him because, well, it was old, dried up and dead and it wouldn't look very nice in either of our houses and you can't grip on to everything he had touched and loved; especially when their attachment to it was partially down to dementia and head injury.

For the time being we mainly put everything into bags to take home and deal with later as Mum was quite flustered and it was difficult for me to answer the questions she was throwing at me. Then she opened a drawer and started giggling and held up a tube of ointment and said, "This was for his itchy testicles." She giggled a bit more, then said with complete sincerity, "Do you think your Dad would want this?" I replied slowly, enunciating clearly to make sure she understood the lunacy of her question, "Are you asking me if I would know if my father would want ointment for his itchy scrotum? Ointment, bearing in mind, that belongs to my recently deceased stepfather?" At this point a silly smirk started to spread across my mother's face and with her eyes glossy with mirth she responded "Ppffftttt... Yes." She stood up straight as if to cement her response as serious before flopping down onto fits of laughter on the bed again. We laughed hysterically for a good five minutes and thoroughly shook the air clean of any tense and stressed energy and left shortly afterwards with our laughing bouncing around Room Six as we closed the door behind us for the very last time.

We went home in separate cars. Mum kept the ointment for an itchy scrotum, I am sure she offered it to every male acquaintance she had with honest concern and proper discretion.

The weeks leading up to the funeral were busy with choosing photos that we all approved of for the order of service and perfecting the wording. All of us needed to find a black outfit for the day and decide what was best to do with the cremation, as the church and the hall for the service and the wake were in the same place and quite far from the crematorium. It was decided to have a small cremation with the coffin and just close friends and family and that the church service would be open to all. We decided to have things that symbolised Geoff on a table by the altar and then all mooch over to the village hall for the wake. We all decided upon the songs that mattered and Mum wanted to make sure there were place settings so the family could sit down and did test runs to see how many we could fit to a pew comfortably. Everything was organised within an inch of its life.

The day before the funeral, the undertaker called me to say that they had finally got Geoff back if I wanted to see him. I had really wanted to go and check he was alright but it had been over two weeks since he had died and I know how the body can change and I also knew how badly it had affected me seeing him going through 'the death rattle'; in fact my mind had blocked it out. I could hear the rasps and see his eyes and teeth but separately, never all at once. It took nearly two years before I got back the memory and it is still only in flashes, as though my head knows I am not ready to remember it all again. The undertaker was very kind and said he would wait until the end of the day to 'put the final nails in the coffin'. That made me feel shaky. He said that he couldn't close his eyes and mouth and that they couldn't straighten his legs without breaking them so they would have to put him in a shorter, but deeper coffin so he would fit as he felt he had been through enough and I agreed. I decided I couldn't see him, not twelve hours before I was to stand up at his funeral and speak about him and I didn't want my last image to be of the remains of his body looking so different to the man who helped bring me up. It was the remains of his body too – not him – it was just the outfit he wore his whole life and the life and soul which had resided within it was no longer there.

We were driven in a swanky limo by the kind undertaker; Mum, Charlie, Sally, Kathy, Baby Wilbur and me. We chatted brightly. En route we received messages of love and support from our friends. My wonderful friend Sophie sent me a text telling me she loved me, then seconds later she sent one meant for her boyfriend… followed by a deeply ashamed and apologetic stream of panicked messages. That was the best thing I could have asked for that morning, I had felt so sick and nervous and that made me laugh, a deep belly laugh, it made us all laugh and relax and Geoff would have loved it – he would have really laughed at that. For future reference: Sophie – please always be on hand to send me a text like that when I am on the way to any funeral.

The warm feeling of laughter stayed in the car almost all the way there, then we saw it. There was the hearse with Geoff's coffin lying in it. We had requested that people sent money to Headway Derby rather than flowers as they had been awesome at looking after Geoff and it was a place he had referred to as 'feeling like he was home.' We got out of the car at the crematorium and I watched as they pulled out the coffin which was shorter than Geoff was and very high. I couldn't help but imagine him in there crumpled up with his eyes and mouth open, unable to close, forever thirsty like the last nine days of his life. The grief completely consumed me. I had not been able to cry since he had died but now it came in great waves; the kind of unattractive crying they don't show in films where you can't help the noises that come out of you – all squeaks and honks. Through my tears I saw my Dad and stepmother Sarah come towards me and envelop me into a hug, "Are you alright my darling?" "He's really in there, it's just hitting me." I gurgled. He was; this was the end of Geoff Casboult, he had really gone. After decades of depression and struggle he had finally gone. Was he at peace? I am not a religious person and he was, on and off. Initially he was but then he had lost his faith but then he sort of found it again, depending on his state of mind. He was unclear about his faith but he was unclear about a lot in those final years. I hoped he was at peace. We hoped he had been met by a lolloping Sam. "Hello, old hound" he would have said before giving him a hug, and he would be with his brother again, his brother who he missed so much that he had relived his death daily for two months because the grief was so great. We hope that was where he was now, not the very frail body in the coffin.

The service was short and beautiful. The staff from The Old Lodge came to say goodbye; they couldn't come to Thorpe for the service. Matron said through tears that a lot of their guests were dying at the moment, you could see the weight of each one sitting on her shoulders. It takes an iron core to care and love each person who comes through your doors knowing that, when they leave, it will because they have died. To stay the same kind creature and never hardening to the job. I remain in awe of that wonderful lady.

I spoke a short piece about the little things that will always make us think of Geoff, like the sound of a cat's paws walking across a wooden floor, or a single note from an instrument in an orchestra which he would notice and point out its beauty where it would have been lost in the music to everyone else. As his coffin went into the curtains, we played 'Wonderful Tonight' by Eric Clapton, chosen by Sally. At the second the curtains came round, Baby Wilbur started to grizzle and Kathy didn't know if it was the done thing to feed him at a funeral. We all looked to each other and agreed it was completely fine. I then looked at everyone else who was looking forward and remembered where I was; I looked up just to see the curtain close and the last whisper of the coffin disappear from view. He was gone and I felt relieved that there had been that distraction for that moment. It did really help.

As I have mentioned we are creatures of habit and find great comfort in that. When we were quite young Kathy was given a 'Jem' doll which came with a cassette of funky music sung by 'Jem & the holograms'; a fictional band created especially for the cartoon it was based on, all electric keyboards and crimped hair. As young children do, we liked to listen to that tape a great deal (much to Mum and Geoff's joy) and, somehow, I don't know how, it became tradition to listen to that tape when we drove off the ferry in Cherbourg. Not immediately; we would have to wait until we had driven through the town and up the big hill then we would play it. It consisted of three short songs. Two punchy numbers and a ballad with very high notes that Geoff would try and reach and go all squeaky. The other side of the tape was instrumental so the tradition was to list to the side with the words first, singing along, then listen to the instrumental side and sing along again. When we were driving home in the funeral car Kathy suggested we had one final blast at Jem, for Geoff. The cassette itself was 'somewhere' in Mum's house so we would have to do it without the music. The words all firmly imbedded into our memory we recited all three of those songs with perfect timing, added backing and great volume. After we had finished there was a small moment's silence before the kind undertaker with his broad Derbyshire accent uttered, "Well, it's not the strangest thing I have ever heard in the back of this car." We all laughed. Geoff would have most definitely approved of all that and joined in with the high notes.

There was a little table near the altar at the church where the coffin would normally be. On that table was Geoff's briefcase he loved so much, still housing his dictaphone with his voice recording his last work notes. His cricket ball and his favourite posh shoes he liked to wear after his accident. Things that gave all of us a connection to him. The Derby Bach Choir, with whom Geoff and Mum had sung, stood either side of the table, ready to sing for Geoff. As the church started to fill we stood in our allowed place in the pew and went to sit: the measurements Mum had done were a little off and there was not enough room for a fifth person. Four of us were now sitting cheek to cheek in a row. We sensed her mistake had been in using Charlie, very thin and tall, to mark the place of one person when it took two of her to fit one of my short and fat places. We had to stifle the laughter as Mum, with a stern look and hushed tones said, "Well I measured it – you should all fit – just move up a bit!" It was a good job we were such a close family as we could literally feel each other's breath. Geoff would have laughed at that too.

The church was so full the doors wouldn't close, there were people standing on every part of the floor and outside the door listening in. The vicar made a joke about fire safety and everyone laughed whilst I tried to bury the bitter feeling of wonder as to where these hundreds of people had been for the last few years of his life. The choir sang beautifully and, with each song, Mum got up and sang too. Charlie spoke about memories and I spoke about my time with him after his accident. It mattered to me that people didn't just brush this time under the carpet. It was difficult and scary and he was weird but it all happened and for people to ignore it means it happened for no reason other than to be forgotten. Geoff hated what happened to him, it stripped him of his proud title as a gentleman and to pretend it didn't happen is acting as though we should have been ashamed. I am a firm believer that everything happens for a reason, no matter how horrible, and I was going to make sure that what happened to Geoff would be something that would help other people in his name.

The wake afterwards was very busy and very full of people all laughing and joking. I couldn't breathe and had to sit outside. I sat with my friends Rachel, Laura (who had been my friend since I was little and had grown up with Geoff), Emily and Alexa who I had gone to school with, and Dan. We sat on the bench and looked at the beautiful sky and talked normally. I didn't want the small talk and I found that people were coming up to me to thank me for the support I gave to Geoff and I felt it was their way of alleviating their guilt for not supporting more themselves and that made me angry again. I needed not to feel angry and the guests were just being kind and dealing with everything in their own way and didn't deserve my anger. Sally really helped me understand how it was to be someone who struggled to cope with what she had written about the experience. We all deal with the guilt after someone dies or is ill; even if you are there every day, or not at all, you deal with regret. It is very easy to say there are no regrets because there, inevitably, must be some.

After the majority of people had left, I went back in and we laughed about how Kathy had got her boobs out almost every time the vicar

opened his mouth to speak so that she could feed Wilbur. Our old
school teacher, with whom we had had always remained close, chatted
to us fondly and Will and Sue were there with us until the end, as they
had always been, quietly helping and knowing exactly what to say. At
the end when we had all said goodbye and Mum had punched everyone out of the door (doing her impressions of when Geoff had got a bit
'fisty cuffy' towards the end) I went home too. I decided to go home,
back to my house that Geoff had never seen, but had photos of all over
his room of because he had always shown an interest in our lives and
had really cared. He was so happy that I had made such a settled life
for myself after being lost for so long – I am so glad he got to see that
before he died.

The front of Geoff's order of service. The snowy view taken by Charlie on the morning of his death.

Geoff's battered old briefcase which he loved so dearly.

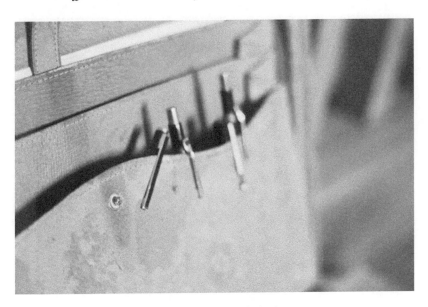

The pens as he had left them.

Geoff's battered old briefcase which he loved so dearly.

His work notepad left with work still incomplete.

McDonalds stickers he was collecting for a free coffee.

His aged dictaphone we used to play with as
children still has his voice on it.

His diary.

14.

It's lonely

========

UNTIL this point, I had only experienced grief that ended with the day of the funeral. That was when you all paid your respects; you laughed and you cried and heaved it all out of your system. Then you felt better and got on with your life, thinking of the person occasionally when their birthday came round or something triggered a memory. The first time you lose someone big is quite a shock. For me, the grief seemed to wait until the funeral and then emptied itself onto me the day after. It's not in little drips either; it is great vats of doughy mixture landing on your head and weighing heavily at the pit of your stomach.

Conveniently, this also seems to be the time that a lot of people quickly lose interest. They have done their grieving, don't need to be reminded of the death anymore and want to carry on. I have always gone by my mother's rule of treating people how you want to be treated, so I have always done little things, like send postcards and letters because I love to get them. In the years prior to Geoff's death, a couple of my friends had the misfortune of losing someone extremely close to them (a husband for one and a mother for another). My thoughts were to just go around as normal and be normal and talk about the people they lost if they wanted to but not ignore their existence altogether. Most people who have lost someone end up with the box of their remains after cremation - a mother in the cupboard, a dad on the kitchen window-sill; people who haven't lost someone find this morbid and frightening; those who have find it a comfort, and sometimes amusing.

I found this time the worst I had ever felt. Dan had to go back to work and the grief was drowning me. Occasionally people would text me asking if I was ok and I would respond with, "No, I am not. I am really struggling." Very few offered to come round and see me and just be normal. It felt like my grief frightened people away. Some friends who I thought to be good friends vanished out of my life completely and friends who I thought to just be acquaintances proved themselves to be kindred spirits. It was then I realised how much death frightens everyone.

The worst experience I had was with University. I had been offered a place at every university I had applied for and I had chosen this one because of its good reviews. When Geoff had his second stroke, they said they would support me and I still came in to almost every lecture. I chose not to mention anything to the students until they asked. When they did ask they reacted as I feared they would - they instantly and physically stepped away from me. Just one, a young man called Mark, pulled his chair to my desk and asked me about Geoff and how I was doing. The rest stopped talking to me altogether but I would catch them looking at me all the time, as though expecting me to start screaming or something.

I was permitted two weeks leave after Geoff had died. I came back to university to find my coursework damaged with an offensive note scrawled over it. Everyone in my group was in the room and just sat there in silence as I looked at what had been done. I turned to face them and none of them would look at me. I was so furious and devastated and completely confused that I walked out and didn't go back.

I went to meet with my tutor two days later. He seemed nervous of me from the second I came into the room. He was handling me like a bomb that was about to go off with both a patronising and terrified tone. His view on things was that we were all adults and it wasn't his place to either stop them from doing it, nor punish them for it and it should be dealt with between us. "You haven't lost anyone yet, have you - both your parents are alive?" I asked him. "Yes, you are right. No one very close to me has died." I realised then that he was as uncomfortable as the students out there. That no one had known what to do so they just all found it easier to try and scare me off. I said that I could only think about Geoff and what had happened at the end, how we had been treated and how I had watched him die. He perked up at that point and said "What *is* 'the death rattle' exactly? How does it sound?", his face focused and hungry. "It's terrifying and horrible." I responded.

His interest was lost after that and it was very clear from the way he was talking that he didn't want me there any more; it felt like no one did. This horrible thing that had happened to me was too uncomfortable for everyone to bear so they wanted me gone rather than have to face it. All it would have taken was normal chatter and a welcome back cake - I didn't want to show them pictures of my dead parent and make them listen to morbid poetry or anything. I was treated like I had the plague and they all wanted me gone as quickly as possible. The tutor made excuses as to why I should 'maybe take a year out': "You won't get your First now, no one has ever got a First here who didn't live in the city. Maybe you could take a year out and then move to the city and start again; you have already passed your first module so you wouldn't have to redo that bit. You can never come back in now as you have missed so much." "I have only missed two weeks and I own my house where I live," I responded, feeling confused and a bit bombarded. [NP]"Well, you weren't *really* here for the weeks before, you only came to lectures. You didn't stay for added studio time; you will never make it up, you will never get your First now."

It was evident that I made him jumpy and he would do everything to get me out. I decided that it would be a decision I would have to make - not them - and I told him that I wanted a list of what was imperative for me to pass this module and carry on as normal. I left clutching my impossible list knowing that I would never return but wanting that to be my decision. One student passed me on the way out. I had only spoken to her once in my time. She said she heard what had happened and hugged me - she smelt like clothes that had been left to dry in a heap and warm body odour but it didn't matter, it was the warmest contact I had received whilst being there.

I had been made to feel like an over-dramatic, skiving, under-acheiver. I felt let down and hurt. I had worked so hard to get to that point in my life (University) and it hadn't been easy. I had been so proud of myself. My family had all been so proud too and now I felt like I was letting them all down by deciding not to go back. I e-mailed the secretary the next day saying I was removing myself and that I was not happy with how I had been treated; she apologised and I could tell that she meant it.

Some months later, after we had met with the hospital about our case, I contacted the secretary again and told her that our case had been referred to as 'one of the worst they had ever dealt with' and that what had happened to me had been proved to be utterly hor-rific. I told her that the way I had been treated at that university was despicable, that I was not even offered support or help, that I was spat on after experiencing something so devastating. The secretary sheep-ishly responded that they had realised after I had gone how badly I was dealt with so they had a seminar that everyone had to attend. I could just imagine them all sat there smirking and joking because they didn't want to deal with the reality that everyone had behaved so shamefully towards me. All but two people who'd simply hugged me and just chatted normally.

At that point I decided that something needed to be done about this; there needed to be more awareness about death which is ludi-crous if you think about it, as death is one of the few things we can be certain of in life; it is inevitable and unavoidable and we should not fear it or those who have experienced it. In Harry Potter, J K Rowling's depiction of being able to see the Thestrals once you have experienced death yourself is how I felt. As if you are made to feel like you are sud-denly carrying around this great dark beast and no one wants to see it. I wanted to normalise death and try and take the fear away from it. I wanted to educate companies and schools with the best way to deal with someone who has lost someone close to them, integrating the correct support and training staff how to best cope and deal with it. A great friend of mine lost her mother when she was nine; when Mother's Day came along they ask all the children to make a card for their mums and she said "What do I do? My mum is dead." The teacher responded that she should just sit this lesson out. What an awful thing to say to a little girl who has lost a parent. Surely she could suggest making one to whomever she wanted would be kinder, including her mother, despite the fact that she is dead, rather than push her away from the class and make her feel even more different and separate.

Something had to be done, as I did not want anyone to experience the humiliation and loneliness that I experienced as a result of lack of understanding and fear. Less than a century ago we would bring the dead back home so that everyone could say goodbye. Their bodies lay in rest in the living room. It is now more our culture to fear death and the people it has touched. There is no understanding of grief and how it affects people. The overriding 'stiff upper lip' attitude creates a feeling of ineptitude to the person who has just lost a great love when they should be spoken of and remembered so the integration back into reality is warmer.

I was left reeling from my experience with the University, so Dan offered to take me away anywhere I wanted and I chose Erquy. After Mum's house had undergone so many changes and shifts to accommodate Geoff post-accident only for him to have to go to The Old Lodge, it had been left incomplete in so many ways and no longer looked or smelled like our childhood home. I felt lost. I needed to feel centred and safe and Erquy was my home - it had not changed in 25 years and housed the smells and memories of my past. We booked the next available boat and went out, out of season to the dormant old familiar fishing town. It was cold and quiet and as we opened up the shutters and woke up our sleepy house I knew I had made the right decision.

In the house I was able to look through 'the red books' and relive our holidays past. I was consumed with sadness and upset. It would take over me a few times a day leaving me with great heaving sobs whilst Dan would just cuddle me. We stayed for 5 days and played cards, drank wine and I cried about everything. I told Dan stories of my past as I remembered them and he listened politely even though I knew he had heard them all before and he made me laugh. Old friends Pascal and Nicole, who we had known forever, came to dinner. I cooked them a proper English roast with all the trimmings and we drank wine and laughed. It was fond company, fine wine and comfort - it was exactly what I had needed. The way I had been treated by everyone at the University had crumbled my barriers that I had worked so hard to keep strong whilst Geoff was ill - you have to form a hard shell to get through the difficult things in life so you don't crumble and that experience of unkindness very nearly broke me. It didn't though. I returned back from Erquy feeling rejuvenated and ready.

15.

The Complaint

GROWING up with a father in the medical profession I was always painfully aware of the pressure that doctors are under and how over-worked all of the medical staff are. With that in mind I would not visit the GP until I was at the point of no return (leg hanging off, death's door etc) and usually this was after I had called my dad or sister to check that I wasn't going to be wasting anyone's time. That being said I was also taught the importance of the job working in medicine and that you should not work there any more if you lose your ability to care about the people you are looking after.

What we experienced in the hospital those last few weeks of Geoff's life was not good medical practice. It was not good human practice. It had left a crushing dent in my life that I would never be able to straighten out and I felt I had to do something to move on. Mum, Kathy and I all decided that we would all write a complaint from each of our own perspectives and send them in together. Mum's covered the entire stay at the hospital which she had documented daily with times and doctors' names; Kathy's came from the perspective of a doctor who knew and understood the correct protocol for end of life care and felt real concern for the way Geoff's case was carried out, while mine was from the record of that day that we tried to get Geoff home.

It mattered to us all that it was done properly and directed to the right people. So often people just shout at the staff at the bottom of the pecking order who have no power to do anything, are often the ones most overworked and who have no responsibility for the decisions made. We spoke with my father about the correct way to deal with the complaint and asked him to read the letter I wrote to check it was right. It mattered that I got my point across without sounding frantic and bitter – it was a very good idea for me to have taken that break away, to step back from the situation and breathe a bit. It took five months actually before it was finally written and sent. To make the full impact we sent the complaint to a number of places so it was really seen. It worked. Within a week we had a response – from everyone. A meeting was set for a few weeks later at the hospital.

Kathy made sure she was free to come too and she brought Baby Wilbur with her. We met with Dr Scott, the head nurse and the sister of the ward who was on annual leave during our time there. We were firstly met with an apology. It was a heartfelt apology meant by every person there. As I mentioned in the last chapter we were told this was one of the worst cases they had recorded and I received a personal apology for what I was put through on that day. We were very clear that we did not want people to be disciplined for their behaviour as it was evident that it was fear and lack of confidence leading to the malpractice and a punitive approach would only increase fear and nervousness throughout the hospital. We wanted more training, more knowledge, more involvement and explanation for the family members. We worried deeply for the families who didn't have the experience of hospitals that we did or a family member who was a GP to hand to explain everything that was happening and tell us that what we were feeling was just. We wanted to help the hospital so that no other family would ever experience what we did. At no point was any kind of monetary compensation discussed; that was not what we wanted from an already struggling NHS. That is something people do not realise when they complain and want compensation; that there is a pot that it comes from and that pot pays the nurses. In some situations money *is* the answer (neglect leading to loss of earnings etc) but this was not the case in our situation. We wanted for it to never happen again and from people to learn from what had happened. I concluded by saying that what I wanted that day was for someone to believe me and to listen and respect us and that you can never underestimate the power of kindness and manners – that statement hung in the air and left a mark and that was exactly what we wanted.

They asked our permission to use our case study for staff to learn how to better deal with their patients and families. We gladly obliged. I was so glad Kathy had bought Wilbur along, aside from the much needed cuddle from him when I burst into tears feeling overwhelmed; it also added a delicious comedy charm when the doctor went to shake our hand when leaving and stepped on one of Wilbur's toys omitting a loud *HONKA* accompanied by a very serious expression on his face. Geoff really would have loved that.

COMPLAINT

> 11 Church Street
> Fritchley
> Nr Belper
> Derbyshire
> DE56 2FQ
> Monday 20 May 2013

To Whom It May Concern:

I am writing to inform you about the unfortunate events which occurred at your hospital in the weeks leading to the death of my stepfather, Geoff Casboult.

Geoff suffered from brain damage following a fall in September 2008 which left him severely disabled, he also suffered a stroke. Geoff was brought into Derby City hospital on 1 January 2013 after, what was later found to be, a second stroke and heart attack. This stroke had caused him to have quite severe and distressing seizures every five to ten minutes which lasted a few minutes and seemed to cause him a lot of discomfort and pain. To stop this he was given a large dose of anti seizure medication which stopped them from happening. At this point he was moved onto ward 410 where he remained for the rest of his stay.

During this time he maintained an unresponsive state and tests showed that he would not recover from this and that we would have to make the decision on the best way to let him die. This is itself was a decision that was incredibly difficult for my mother, my sisters and myself to have to make. We are very fortunate that one of my older sisters is a GP in Newcastle and has a lot of experience in end of life care, so she was able to speak to the doctors in the hospital and ensure that we all completely understood what we were all agreeing to.

It was decided that he would be discharged back to the care home where he had lived since mid 2011 so he would be in the comfort of his own room with nurses and staff who knew him and we would let him die as comfortably as possible, removing the NG tube at the same time. I had requested that I be informed when he was being discharged and transferred as I wanted to go with him so he was not alone (as I had done when he was initially brought in on 1 January).

On Thursday 17 January 2013 I was called by one of the staff at 13:30 saying that his ambulance was due to arrive to transport him at 14:30, I left immediately and got to the ward for 14:00. When I arrived I was shown to a little side room where Geoff was in a bed on his own. The first thing that I noticed was that his eyes were open and he seemed much more alert (see Fig 1 and 2 for comparison pictures, one taken on this day and one two days before) I was told that they had stopped all his medication the previous night so, by that point, he had been given no medication for 24 hours. I noticed that he was looking at me too, when I asked the junior doctor about this he said that it was not so, and that he wasn't really there. He was very polite and said it was a shame but there was ultimately nothing more that could be done.

I have spent a lot of time with Geoff, especially in the last few years since his initial accident, and I recognised that he was not as unresponsive as they first made out. I asked if I could give him any water on a sponge and was told I could do that whenever I wanted and when I did he seemed incredibly thirsty and his eyes were engaged with mine. I decided to text my GP sister as I was not entirely convinced about it. When I spoke with her she was confused as to why he had no saline drip so I went to ask the ward sister who said to me that they were letting him die with no saline, with nothing at all. When I asked why he could not have a drip as he was clearly thirsty I was met with the response, "What's the point?" This was a response I was met with many more times that day and each time I heard it, it devastated me. It is very difficult hearing that someone you love does not appear to matter.

Around 15:30 Geoff seemed to be in discomfort and pain; I called the nurse to ask if he could get some kind of pain relief and she said that she would ask what he is allowed as he had been taken off everything. Again I mentioned that he definitely seemed much more alert and that he could hear me and see me, I was led to believe that I was imagining things as it may be what I wanted to see. I can assure you, I never wanted to see Geoff in clear distress and fear, I never wish to see anyone like that again but unfortunately I will never be able to forget it.

I continued to ask for pain relief as the evening went on and was told that they weren't sure what he was allowed and that also no one else had heard him cry out. At around 17:00 I took out my mp3 player and played Geoff one of his favourite songs. I had done this every day since 1 January when I came to visit him as I wanted him to hear something he loved. Every day I had no response at all from him, on this day he burst into sobbing tears and it sounded like he was trying to say something to me. He kept full eye contact and was clearly very upset. I could not make out any of the words he was trying to say. I told him what was happening and that he was going back to the care home and that we were trying to make him as comfortable as possible and that I loved him, at that point his cries turned more into howls. It was very clear to me that he could understand and the worst part of it is that I do not know if he was trying to tell me that he didn't want to go that way and that he was not ready to die.

At this point my boyfriend came to join me after work and found me in an extremely distressed state and he was able to witness Geoff's cries. He also agreed that he was more alert and appeared to understand. My boyfriend knew Geoff well and was also very close to him. My sister called to see what was happening as she seemed very angry that he hadn't been transferred and that nothing was done about his pain relief and that he did not have any of the medication needed for the end of life pathway; she also felt he needed reassessing. Having heard his cries over the phone she was not happy that he was in the vegetative state that the staff claimed he was in. As horrible as it was for us all, I am greatly relieved that my sister and my boyfriend were able to witness this with me as I was made to feel like I had been making it all up. I cannot express how heartbreaking it is to see someone you love so scared and upset and being told by the professionals around you that you are imagining it.

Eventually, at around 19:30, they administered two parac-etamol to Geoff anally. I thought this was a little odd as I didn't think someone who was supposed to be dying would be given paracetamol as pain relief and administered in such a way seemed slightly degrading. When I explained this to my sister she was out-raged and asked me to speak to the head nurse about it. When I did speak to him, he said he would pull up his notes on the computer to see what his plan was, only to say that he was being sent home with nothing at all and that there was nothing on his notes. At this point my sister requested to talk to him. He claimed that he was not allowed to prescribe Geoff any kind of stronger medication and my sister pointed out that he was on an end of life plan and that he was able to. At the end of the conversation he was clearly annoyed and handed me back the phone and walked off without explaining anything to me. After that the staff talked about Geoff in hushed tones around the corner from us and would not let me know what they were saying when I asked.

At one point a cleaner came in to empty the bins and tidy the room, she did not speak to us or acknowledge we were there, 30 minutes after that I walked around Geoff's bed as it had started snowing and I wanted him to see, when I got round there I noticed the cleaner had emptied the bin onto the floor and left the contents there. This, to me, felt completely disrespectful to us and symbolic of how we were perceived; like a room full of rubbish. I asked the nurse for it to be cleared up and it was after a while.

As the night went on the ambulance still hadn't arrived and Geoff was still crying out in pain and distress. I asked why the ambulance had not come and was told that there were a lot of peo-ple being discharged today, I responded by pointing out that Geoff was end of life and had been waiting since 14:00 so perhaps he would get to be one of the first, again I was met with the same, "what's the point?" comments. At one point I heard the head nurse saying that he was just going to leave Geoff here overnight and get a transfer in the morning, at this point I said that was unacceptable and had been given no medication and was in clear distress and that he needed to be back where he felt at home.

At around 21:30 a new head nurse came on; she did listen to me and agreed that Geoff should have diamorphine and that she would arrange for this. Keeping in contact with my sister she informed me that he would need to have medication to take home with him for his end of life plan and I needed to make sure he got that. At 22:00 we were told that the ambulance was coming, Geoff still had no pain relief and nothing to take back with him. I voiced that, since the ambulance was so busy, that we could not keep them waiting once they got here so everything would need to be done immediately. At that point, finally, the new head nurse gave him the diamorphine, she said that there wouldn't be time to get the rest of his medication so I offered to drive and collect it and bring it back to his care home to which she agreed.

The ambulance arrived at roughly 22:30, I walked with him to the ambulance and then followed in my car. As I got to my car the head nurse called to say I couldn't pick up his pain relief as it was diamorphine and it was not allowed as I was not a medical professional and that it would be sent in a taxi the following morning.

When I got to the care home I was greeted by one of the nurses who knew him, she was not happy that he did not have anything with him for pain relief throughout the night. When I went into his room he seemed so much more relaxed and I sat with him for a while and he just looked at me. He looked incredibly sad.

The following day the Matron at the care home called to say that she too did not think he was end of life and did not feel right about starving him of water and nutrients. It took a few days to get it but by Tuesday 22 January he was finally given a saline drip. He had been without one since the evening of Wednesday 16 January.

He passed away in the early hours of Saturday 26 January, due to the heavy snow I was not able to be with him when he passed which upset me deeply. I have no illusions that he was going to live for years or even months more but I know that he could have been looked after much better. I cannot even try to explain the trauma I have felt as a result of this whole ordeal. He was my parent and a very important person in my life and I worked hard to make sure he was not suffering only to be made to feel like I was imagining his reactions or told "what's the point?". That sentence I will never be able to forget or his cries. I will never be able to forgive myself for not pushing more with the nurses and stopping his distress, I will always feel that I let him down and that is something I will have to live with for the rest of my life.

I am incredibly lucky to have a sister who is a qualified and experienced physician, without her I do not know how I would have coped. It was with her knowledge and support that I was even able to get Geoff home that night, all I can think about is the families who do not have that knowledge and support, are they made to feel like they are imagining things too? Are they also asked; "what is the point?' about someone they love? The thought of it terrifies me.

I have always respected people who work within the medical profession; but this was not respectful towards us and it was made clear that Geoff was not someone worth wasting time on. I just hope that he could not understand what was going on around him as, more than anything, he would not want his children to have to experience such a dreadful thing. It was unjust, disrespectful and unacceptable. Something needs to be done about this so that no one else has to experience what we experienced.

Sincerely
Annie Fielder

Copies of this complaint also sent to local MP Margaret Beckett, Royal Derby Hospital Chief Executive Mrs Susan D. James, Geoff Casboult's consultant Dr Scott and Derby City Patient Participation Group.

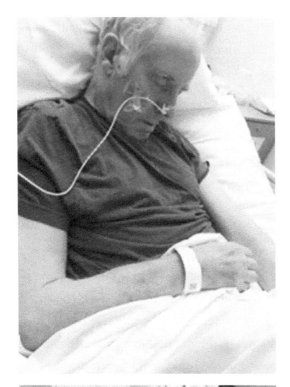

Fig 1.

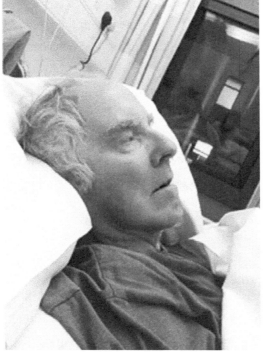

Fig 2.

16.

The Exhibition

===========

WITH the anniversary of Geoff's death looming I decided to exhibit the project that he and I had done together (originally for my university project) as a distraction for me. Having raised over a thousand pounds from the collection at Geoff's funeral for Headway Derby we decided it would be good to exhibit it there and raise more money for them at the same time. I had two further pictures made explaining that he had died as we finished the project in 2012.

Dan and I had recently got engaged and had decided to try for a family. From a young age I had been told that having children naturally was 'unlikely' and 'difficult' but we had to try before being considered for alternative options. Feeling very unwell that entire month but convincing myself it was worry with the stress of Geoff's death-aversary coming up or a virus I pushed back thoughts of a child, plus that was the first month we had started trying. The weekend of the exhibition we found out I was pregnant. We all decided it was a gift from Geoff, he knew how much I had wanted to be a mother. Oddly, the November before he died, he said to me; "and you're pregnant aren't you?" and I said "No Geoff – *Kathy* has just had a little boy." he replied; "I know but you are having a little boy too aren't you?" I definitely wasn't pregnant at the time but I was now and I was carrying a little boy. The distraction of pregnancy really helped me through that month and I didn't buckle once, in fact it pushed me further as something I never thought could ever happen was happening and I know that would have made Geoff so happy.

The exhibition went perfectly. We supplied more bottles of Costco's best Cava than one could shake a stick at (which remained untouched as everyone wanted to focus on the exhibition – we ended up handing it out to friends as they left) and we raised just under £400 in the four hours that it showed. The impact it had surprised me. Geoff's old Speech Therapist became overwhelmed and had to take time out and when I went to speak to him, it was him who gave me the nudge to write this book and who wrote the beautiful testimonial. I realised that everything we had done from the start really could make a difference and should. That everything we all went through could be used to help others so that is what I decided to do.

17.

Strength and Support

================

IT is important to take time out for the people who were amazing throughout this time in our lives because a good amount of people quickly dissipated only to briefly reappear for the funeral which infuriated me. There are two people I want to take note of; my mother and her friend and neighbour Will Smith. Firstly mother.

A great force of a human being, our Mother. Kindness that knows no boundaries with a contrasting, overpowering sense that she will only be herself and, as long as it is not hurting anyone, she will not change who she is, that is to say, deliciously bonkers…, a snappy dresser, a lover of all things French including 'proper coffee', always late but with a fantastically descriptive and ludicrous story as to why – with onomatopoeic grunts and huge hand gestures , a mother to anyone who needs it, <u>loves</u> laughing, loves teaching, loves the colours when it is about to rain and the sun is shining but the skies are really dark and makes the best gravy ever in existence (and will fight you tooth and nail for the last dregs in the gravy dish.)

Throughout my life I always felt completely supported by my mother. If anyone of us had come home with our heads shaved, tattooed blue and announcing we were marrying an avocado she would support us, as long as we were happy – she would laugh – but she would support us. I remember meeting my mother in Ashbourne as a teenager and seeing her walking from quite far off before she saw me, she walked slower than everyone else and her resting face was that of a calm smile. People reacted by smiling at her and her smile then broadened. I remember looking at my reflection in a window and a young girl with a furrowed brow looked back. From then on I tried to smile all the time like she does – the wrinkles that have formed between my brow some 19 years later are living proof that I was unsuccessful in that quest.

Before Geoff's accident, when his depression was at its highest point, my mother always remained cheerful. I can remember calling the house and Mum answering brightly; "Oh hello! Geoff hasn't spoken a word to me for three weeks and Sally is hiding in her room. I'm listening to the radio – put on Classic FM now! Listen to those drums *BOOM BOOM BOOM CRASH!* Isn't it incredible? I can remember singing this in a thunderstorm, it was breathtaking!" Never a snifter of woe in her voice or attitude and this has continued on throughout her life.

Do not read this wrong – she was never a woman in denial and, if needing to cry or get cross she did, but she did not wallow about things that had or were happening to her. She felt very real sadness for us girls and felt it very deeply but she didn't dwell on her own misfortune ever, there was always something beautiful or silly to be marvelled at.

At one point in the hospital, Geoff was in ICU and we were ushered into a little room to wait for some results about something serious, I forget now as they all seem to have amalgamated into one. We were all sitting on those uncomfortable 'comfortable' chairs they have in those hospital room and Mum was gazing around with her usual smile and then saying; "Oh Lawks! Do you have a pen?!" turning to look we saw that, on the arm of the chair Mother was on was crudely drawn male genitalia. Using her artistic skills she expertly remodelled it into a little man's face. "There – no one will ever know now." Then the doctor walked in and she stood up to greet him.

Throughout the time following Geoff's accident he pointed his anger and poison to Mum and myself – but to Mum mostly, she always got the brunt of it and we would often remind him that he used to be a gentleman once. Mum rarely reacted and would just shrug her shoulders or laugh, she knew it wasn't about her but sometimes she would let it upset her. It wasn't nice, what was happening.

During the time when Geoff's mania hit, her beloved father, our wonderful Grandpa, died. He was 92 and we had just discovered that he had liver cancer. He wasn't in any pain and was very old and completely happy with life and died peacefully lying in bed next to Granny. Due to Geoff's state of health and mind, Mum didn't really get time to mourn her dad who was the most magical person of all. He used to invent little things like a tiny lamp so that Mum could see the fairies as a little girl and the machine to distract frightened children in his dental office of a fox chasing a rabbit that used to dart from wall to wall so he could work on their teeth without them really noticing. He had a smile that would light up a whole country (the very same smile Mum has) and twinkly blue eyes. My little boy has his eyes and that makes me so happy to see him in there. Grandpa had a joke he would tell – it was a little dated. It went like this:

"A man with a wooden leg went to stay in a hotel. When he went for his dinner the concierge asked if he would like a bed pan to warm his bed to which he replied 'Yes'. Later on in the evening the concierge realised that he had forgotten to take the bed pan out of the man's bed – so he crept up to his room, slowly reaching into the bed to retrieve the handle of the bed pan and then crept out again. When walking back down the stairs he realised that in his hands was not the bed pan, but the man's wooden leg."

That is it. That is the entire joke. I can honestly say that I never heard my Grandpa finish that joke. I don't think I ever heard him get past the point where the concierge realised that he'd forgotten to take the bed pan out. He would be totally incomprehensible. His glasses would be off and he would be dabbing his tear-soaked cheeks with his handkerchief and rocking from side to side with uncontrollable mirth. None of us ever found the joke remotely funny but I cannot think of anything funnier than watching him tell it then us needing about twenty minutes to bring him round again which was always followed with periodic guffaws as he remembered the funny bit again and he would be off. We often tell Mum she looks and acts like Grandpa and she clutches her chest and throws her head back as though suddenly enveloped with a warm light and says "Thank you."

When Mum lost her dad she went to seek help with Cruse Bereavement Care and talked to someone about the loss of Grandpa. At that time she also started to talk about the loss of Geoff, not just from the accident but before, when she lost him to depression. Geoff's head injury was in 2008 but it was 1994 when his depression really started to consume our home and Mum lost the man she had married. They had married in 1986; that is eight years of happiness before things turned dark and through the darkness there was always a little safe, warm glow radiating from my mother. I like to think that the strength I have is from her.

Will Smith has been a neighbour of Mum and Geoff's since we moved to the village in 1986. We had always known him and his lovely wife Sue and they had come to all our family shindigs and knees ups. When Geoff was first ill everyone who knew him, pretty much, came to visit him and offered help. When people realised that he wasn't getting better and began to understand the longevity of his illness there was an instant decline in visitors with most people stopping all together and the rest reducing both their amounts of visits and the length of time they would visit for – starting each visit with; "I can only pop in for a second as there is something in the oven." or, "I can't stay long, I have to go and pick up *insert child/friend/pets name here* in twenty minutes." I understood that it was difficult for some people to come because Geoff wasn't Geoff anymore, but he knew who people were and he had always been a loyal friend.

The thing is that some people are copers and some people are not and it *is* uncomfortable and unpleasant when someone you have known well starts shouting and crying in front of you but as human beings you do adapt quickly to your new environment. It would always take me by surprise when Geoff would suddenly roar or swear. It didn't seem to bother Will though. When Geoff became worse he came round more and asked to learn how to use the hoist so that Mum could go out of the house still. He would come round and play dominoes with Geoff and listen to him.

At this point we had to take the Weeto phone away from Geoff as he was calling people in the middle of the night saying he had died and he wanted to say goodbye to them, including the police. He had this new obsession that he was dead. Will was not affected by any of this. Once Geoff was moved to The Old Lodge, Will continued to visit a few times a week right until the very end. The morning Geoff died, the night of the biggest snowfall, Mum looked out of her window to see that Will was clearing the snow from her steps and driveway. By the time she had dashed downstairs he had gone again.

We would have struggled without Will's constant and unwavering support. He was incredibly kind to us all and normal with Geoff, even when Geoff was strange. His warm heart and support was something that helped carry us all the way past the end. Will is not a man who takes gratitude well and would often disappear like a flash whenever we tried to thank him for everything. He doesn't like to do things to be thanked he does them because he genuinely enjoys helping people. We need to thank you though, Will, so when you read this (and I know you will as you continue to support our family even now) thank you so much from the very bottom of our hearts – you made our lives better, you made everything easier and you helped Geoff and were the greatest friend to him that he could ever ask for. You are a good and kind soul and I will always be thankful that you were in our lives during this time. Please accept our thanks, please accept my thanks because I really need to say it to you – you wonderful man.

Mum and Geoff on her 60th birthday weekender.

Mum with her glittery cardboard cut out of the Queen she likes to bring to most fancy social occasions. My mother in a nutshell: smiling, kind, strong, totally reliable (although sometimes a bit late) and totally hilarious.

18.

Whiffle Pig

===

THIS company was started to work as some distraction for my good friend and soon to become loyal business partner Rachel following the quick and surprising death of her lovely mother after a short illness. The word 'Whiffle Pig' was used as a term of endearment between us when the other was feeling sad, it would give each other an instant boost. It meant that when ever we mentioned our company name it would follow with a feeling of warmth, and, when explained, left warmth behind for others.

Following what happened to Geoff it was Rachel's turn to comfort and carry me as I had done with her less than a year earlier with her mother and we carried each other. We had always wanted to keep the ethos of our business as pushing the boundaries of imagination, laughter and helping people. I wanted to use this to help people in similar positions to us. Having worked, voluntarily, in the art therapy sector for over a decade I approached local charities offering our time and experience for free workshops.

My plan, when at University, was to follow my Fine Art BA with an Art Therapy MA but, due to the way I had been treated I had to put that plan aside. I was informed by a nice lecturer upon leaving that I may be eligible to go straight to the MA due to my experience and age – so that will be my future plan. For now it will be to offer what I do have: compassion, kindness, creativity and experience.

We started working with Making Space Derby with elderly folks with dementia and their partners. It mattered to me that the carers were involved too and they often got quite carried away with their projects while we talked to their partners. Next we spoke with The Derby Women's Centre and started confidence building workshops for the ladies with mental health issues there, then we set up workshops with Headway Derby as I was keen to give something back to them for what they had done for Geoff.

Each of our workshops worked with the same concept loosely based on the Froebel Method of using creative play and responding to the person rather than setting something out for people to do and making them do it. We always started our workshops by coming in and talking to each person, keeping the groups small at no more than six people (excluding carers) so that we could take time to listen to each person patiently and gauge what makes them tick. We always introduce music; it calms people and ignites memories. The first workshop is always about learning from the people who have come to it and then shaping the future workshops around them so that we can bring the best of them out in a way that makes them feel comfortable and safe.

In my experience of working voluntarily I often found the classes and workshops to be restrictive and often, rather childlike and patronising. This was something I wanted to step away from. Alongside all neurological illnesses walks a deep self-awareness that you are not the same as you were and you make mistakes. Often, once diagnosed, the people around you tend to talk to you differently and become untrusting of your state of mind and things you say, making you, yourself, have self doubt and a loss of identity. This sort of behaviour can speed up the effects of these illnesses such as dementia and Parkinson's, or stop the rehabilitation process of something like a head injury or stroke with the patient losing confidence in their own thought process and memory.

What we wanted to do was to use simple ways to bring those people back. Even with the dementia patients who no longer spoke there was always some way to stimulate them. We brought a box of old fabric scraps and buttons that one lovely lady would sink her hands into and smile and laugh whilst her husband and carer would paint and sing and tell us stories of their past and their lives before she was ill. All too often patients are seen as taking up a bed and old people are not respected for the people they used to be and still are. Repsecting these people matters, and what we are trying to do is give them back a small zest to their lives.

Shortly after the exhibition we met with Laura Waters of 'Air Arts for Wellbeing' based in the Derby Royal Hospital, who was really interested in the work we had been doing and I was keen to be working within the hospital where Geoff had been. It was decided that we would run a few months worth of sample sessions to see how we would fit and if it would work. It was at this time we realised that we could no longer fund these workshops on our own as, being just two of us, there was no time to make merchandise and bespoke orders to sell to fund the workshops so we would have to apply for funding.

Our workshops started within the hospital this year working on the dementia ward, the FEAT lounge, the Stroke Unit and King's Lodge where Geoff had been. To start the workshops we used the donated materials we had to hand and worked testing the water with the patients to see what worked and what didn't and collected feedback and information. Working in the FEAT Lounge of the Medical Assessment Unit was interesting as the turnaround for the patients there is no more than 24 hours and they are, primarily, the elderly. We asked them to help us make paper and material flowers for visitors to buy for patients as real flowers aren't allowed on many of the wards – the money raised going back into the workshops. We also asked them to knit squares to go to Neonatal for the babies, each with a selection of photographs explaining where they had come from so visitors and patients could see that the hospital was helping itself. This also gave the patients in the FEAT lounge a sense of achievement. One patient had been readmitted the following week and was waiting for us; she had asked to come along to our workshop as she had enjoyed it so much. Our ideas were starting to come into place.

We were granted the first set of funding in 2015, which has set us up for, at least, a further six months of workshops within the hospital. We plan to expand to work in more wards around the hospital. I met with the artistic board at the hospital about the Geoff Project being exhibited again but within the hospital walls. Interestingly, the fact it involved death caused a very strong frightened reaction from two of the board members. This shows me how important it is going to be to do more work helping everyone understand death and grief and to not fear those dealing with it.

What we wanted and do want is to wiggle the barrier between staff and patient, to encourage them to give a piece of themselves to each other to see each other as people again. To help visitors who might ordinarily struggle to see a relative with a difficult illness and help them focus on something different during their stay and strengthening the bond between them. We want to alleviate the boredom often felt in hospital by the patients by helping them to entertain themselves and give themselves the opportunity to achieve projects and accomplishments that they may not have thought to do, or not had time to do in their lives before. To take the pressure away from the overworked staff because the patients are calmer and their stays shorter. To give everyone; staff, patients and visitors a time to remember what they used to enjoy before they grew up and became too busy and see that we are all, deep down, the same. Above all, keeping the ethos of kindness and manners and let us not forget laughter.

Geoff told me that he was at peace with everything, about eight weeks before he died, which was refreshing after the years of loud suicide threats. This entire experience was Geoff's worst nightmare and stripped him completely of his proud title of 'Gentleman'. Using his story to help others means there was a reason why this happened to us and the fact that now it has already eased the pain of others is exactly what Geoff would have wanted. I am proud to have been a part of his life and I am happy to keep his name going in our work.

The photoshoot at the end of the dressmaking workshops with our designer friend Fazane Malik (top left) who kindly helped us for free, Rachel, the other half of Whiffle Pig (second from the left, top) and me – far right – seven months pregnant.

*Simple children's workshops Whiffle Pig has run to
raise money to fund the charity workshops.*

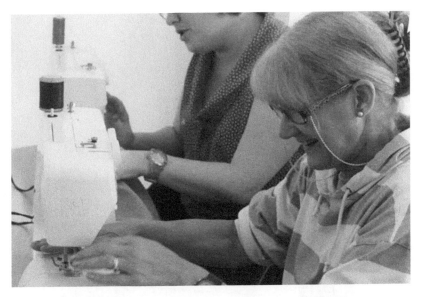

Dressmaking workshops we ran, for free, for the Derby Women's Centre to help with building confidence - teaching them a skill they can continue to use.

Desert Island Discs workshop we did with the chaps at Headway.

Workshops for people with Dementia and their
partners/carers. Christmas decorations workshop.

Important Contacts

WHEN this happened to us we spent a great deal of time looking for help and support so I have compiled some contact details and reading matter to help those who may need it.

Carers advice:
www.carersuk.org 08088087777

www.carers.org 08448004361

www.mind.org.uk 03001233393

www.rethink.org 03005000927

Head Injury and Stroke:
www.headway.org.uk 08088002244

www.stroke.org.uk 03033033100

Dementia and Parkinson's:
www.alzheimers.org.uk 03002221122

www.dementiauk.org 08452579406

www.parkinsons.org.uk 08088000303

Depression and mental illness:
www.makingspace.co.uk 01925571680

www.depressionuk.org

www.helpguide.org

www.samaritans.org 08457909090

www.sane.org.uk   03003047000

Death and grief support:
www.suddendeath.org

www.cruse.org.uk 08444779400

www.deathcafe.com

If you want to properly give feedback to your hospital, whether it be a complaint or thanking a particular member of staff, contact your local PALS (Patient and Liaison Services) and they will be able to help make sure your feedback goes to the right person.

Books which we found helpful:

- *Severe Depression – The Essential Guide for Carers.* Tony Frais.
- *Living with a Black Dog – How to take care of someone with depression while looking after yourself.* Matthew and Ainsley Johnstone.
- *Days With My Father.* Phillip Toledano.
- *Tangles – A story about Alzheimer's, My Mother and Me.* Sarah Leavitt.
- *Michael Rosen's Sad Book.* Michael Rosen.

ND - #0214 - 270225 - C0 - 234/156/8 - PB - 9781780915104 - Gloss Lamination